THE KEYS TO THE
DA VINCI CODE

 SelectBooks

THE KEYS TO THE DA VINCI CODE

THE HIDDEN LINEAGE OF JESUS AND OTHER MYSTERIES

❖

MARIANO FERNÁNDEZ URRESTI
LORENZO FERNÁNDEZ BUENO

 SelectBooks

The Keys to the Da Vinci Code

Originally published as Las claves del Código da Vinci
by Ediciones Nowtilus, S.L. in 2004

Spanish language edition © 2004 by Mariano Fernández Urresti and Lorenzo
Fernández Bueno

This edition © 2006 by Mariano Fernández Urresti and Lorenzo Fernández Bueno
Translated from the Spanish Edition by Rachel Williams for Grupo ROS
Cover design: Carlos Peydró

ISBN 1-59079-101-0

First English language Edition

Library of Congress Cataloging-in-Publication Data has been applied for

Manufactured in the United States of America

10 9 8 7 6 5 4 3 2 1

CONTENTS

To all the men and women who have been persecuted for their ideas and beliefs throughout history. May these lines serve as cold water poured on so many burnings at the stake.

MARIANO FERNÁNDEZ URRESTI

To all the researchers who over the centuries have fallen victim to those who did not grasp knowledge, because this will never be lost.

LORENZO FERNÁNDEZ BUENO

A Cool Head

ON ONE OF THE OCCASIONS WHEN I WAS IN JERUSALEM filming a documentary, I took a detailed tour of the underground passageways and vaults that surround part of the retaining wall holding up the platform of heaped rubble and earth on which the Temple was built. There is nothing special about this since, as the reader knows, the so-called Wailing Wall is the visible part of the aforementioned wall, and at one end is the entrance to the "Tunnel of the Hasmoneans" which leads to these underground passages. The reader will also know that the these ruins are from the Second Temple, built under the reign of King Herod, since the first temple built by King Solomon was destroyed in 586 BC by Nebuchadnezzar's troops. I give these unnecessary explanations because down below in one of the excavated areas several square meters of surface formed by stone slabs have been uncovered, which surrounded the Temple two thousand years ago and which, like many others, Jesus probably walked over. It was here that, running my hand over the smooth slabs with all the delight of those of us who love the past, I became aware of something. In the same way as the real scene of the Passion was buried some twelve or fourteen feet underneath the Via Dolorosa that pilgrims travel today with veneration, the true story of the leader of the "Nazarene Sect" is trapped beneath tons of prejudices and pious falsehoods, the difference being that the latter will never be unearthed.

The Jesus that we know is of the Gospels, as far from the true Jesus as befits an idealized person, with a biography in keeping with His role of Savior. On the other hand, the historical data is irrelevant since, with all due respect to His spiritual values, for His fellow citizens and for historians Jesus almost went unnoticed; He was just another of the many "social agitators" in the convulsed Palestine of the first century. At this stage, it is quite simply impossible to know what the Son of Man was like, what His doubts and aspirations were, His relationship with His friends and family, or whether He lived with anyone at any time. Should the social and political circumstances that made Christianity prosper not have come about, no one would be talking about Jesus today. However, this figure and the religion created around Him are a fundamental referent for hundreds of millions of people around the world, and speculation becomes necessary, however ill- or well-founded, to fill in the gaps in His biography. Consequently, alongside the evangelical Jesus, a legendary Jesus has been developed, even more inapprehensible due to the initiatory nature of the groups that consider themselves repositories of "secrets" about His life, and clearly destabilizing from the point of view of conventional religion. Diving into this ocean of cryptic "truths" without drowning is a difficult feat indeed; as the popular saying goes, one has to keep the head cool and the feet warm. In my opinion, the authors have achieved this and have cleared away all the overgrowth so that readers know what credit to give to the possible bloodline of Jesus, to His "marriage," to His secret zealously guarded by secret societies, and to other highly topical subjects that surround Him.

F. JIMÉNEZ DEL OSO

Some Verbal Brushstrokes

DEAR READER,

I am writing you this letter to express some of your doubts and hesitations out loud. You will quickly discover that I hold nothing certain in my hands and that, just like the air, the figure of Jesus slips right through my fingers. However, I also hope that it serves to warn, without me having to endeavor to prove it, that all of the following ruminations stem from respect for this figure showered with so much attention. In the same way, they are also the result of a certain feeling of indignation towards the only model of thought imposed by others at the expense of that extraordinary man that Jesus must have been.

Taking as a pretext the million-dollar best-seller *The Da Vinci Code*, the chapters that follow aim to trace what truth there might be in those who fuel the stories of the Holy Grail as blood, the product of the supposed descendants of Jesus and Mary Magdalene. Are they stark raving mad or do their suggestions appear to have foundation?

Of course, for them to be so we would have to read what we believe we know about Jesus in quite a different way. For them to be so, firstly we would have to contradict what the Church has presented as articles of faith. For them to be so, we would have to ask ourselves whether we have been conned for two thousand years, no less...

MARIANO FERNÁNDEZ URRESTI

The Past is of No Interest

...is a commonplace that has gone out of the window with this work. The existence of Jesus—His more human side—not only moves us but arouses as many or more passions as His supposed divinity. Indeed, we only have to look at what some publications—some of them specialist, others generalist—have had to say about Dan Brown's polemic work. Few praise the bravery and coherence of the arguments that he disguises as an adventure novel. The majority fiercely criticize a piece of work that has become, whether on its own merit or not we do not know, the principal point of reference when it comes to quoting Jesus of Nazareth's "other life" offered by the apocryphal chronicles, and supported on a very few occasions by the presence of valuable age-old documents. A being who was born to suffer for the sins of humanity may have had an existence that was somewhat different from what the Holy Scriptures recount. Clearly these are speculations, but there is a journalistic principle that states that the rumor is the prelude to the news, and in this case there are too many rumors flying about.

Nonetheless, before dealing with some issues of considerable importance, we should look at some of the comments made about *The Da Vinci Code*. This will help to understand a little better the conflicting feelings that it evokes.

On November 12, 2003, the website e-cristians.com presented its readers with the hard-hitting essay "The Historical Truth Distorted by The Da Vinci Code," displaying its deep sense of unease about the matter: "*The Da Vinci Code* is an anti-Catholic work of fiction that is becoming a best-seller around the globe. With more than 30 million copies sold, translated into 30 languages and with the rights to the film sold to Columbia Pictures and director Ron Howard—with Tom Hanks picked for the starring role—it has already become a mass culture phenomenon ... And the message that the novel transmits is basically the following:

1. Jesus is not God: no Christian believed that Jesus was God until Emperor Constantine deified Him at the Council of Nicea in 325.

2. Mary Magdalene was Jesus' sexual companion; their offspring, carrying His blood, are the Holy Grail—sang real/Santo Grial/Holy Grail—and the founders of the Merovingian dynasty in France, and the ancestors of the novel's protagonist.

3. Jesus and Mary Magdalene represented the duality of masculine and feminine—just like Mars and Athena, Isis and Osiris; Jesus' first followers worshipped the "sacred feminine"; this worship of the feminine is hidden in the churches built by the Knights Templar, in the secret held by the Priory of Sion—of which Leonardo Da Vinci was a member—and in thousands of other hidden cultural codes.

4. The evil Catholic Church invented by Constantine in 325 persecuted the tolerant and peaceful worshipers of the feminine, killing millions of witches during the Middle Ages and the Renaissance and destroying all the Gnostic Gospels that were not to their liking, leaving only the few Gospels that were in their interest in a heavily rewritten version. In the novel, the Machiavellian Opus Dei does its best to prevent the heroes from revealing the secret: that the Grail is in fact the children of Jesus and Mary Magdalene and that the first God of the Gnostic "Christians" was female.

"The novel tries to sell all of the above as academically grounded, historically valid, and reliably documented.

"In an author's note at the beginning of the book, Dan Brown states: 'All descriptions of artwork, architecture, documents, and secret rituals in this novel are accurate.' As we will see, this statement is false: the errors, inventions, distortions, and mere unfounded rumors abound throughout the novel.

"The pretensions to intellectualism are belied by the bibliography he has used: serious history or art books are few and far between in Brown's reference library, whereas parascience, esoterism, and pseudo-history stand out.

"Dan Brown, on his own website, clearly sets out that he has not written a novel full of nonsense just for fun: 'Rumors of this conspiracy have been whispered for centuries. They are not my own.'

"The result has been rocketing sales of pseudohistorical books about the Church, the Gnostic Gospels, women in Christianity, pagan goddesses, etc...The website Amazon.com has been the first to benefit, linking *The Da Vinci Code* to neo-pagan pseudohistory, radical feminism, and new age books. Fiction is the best way of educating the masses, and when it is disguised as science—the history of art and of religions, in this case—it deceives readers even better.

"As the saying goes: 'slander boldly, something always sticks, and if you slander with information that sounds scientific—even if it is made up—it will stick all the more.'"

Did Constantine Invent Christianity?

BROWN'S ENTIRE "HISTORICAL" GROUNDING rests upon one event: the Council of Nicea in 325. According to his theory, before this date Christianity was an open movement that accepted the "divine feminine," did not view Jesus as God, and produced many Gospels. In this year Emperor Constantine, committed to the masculine cult of the

Invincible Sun, suddenly took over Christianity, banished 'the Goddess,' turned the prophet Jesus into a hero/sun god, and started a Stalinist-style raid to wipe out all the Gospels that were not to his liking.

For any reader with the slightest historical knowledge, this theory is absurd for at least two reasons—

1. There are texts that prove that Christianity prior to 325 was not as the novel describes it and that Gnostic texts were as unfamiliar to Christians as new age publications are today: parasitic and external.

2. Even if Constantine had wanted to change the Christian faith in this way, how would he have been able to do it at a council without not only thousands of Christians, but also hundreds of Bishops catching on?

Many of the bishops at Nicea were veterans who had survived the persecutions initiated by Diocletian and carried bodily scars from

prison, torture, or forced labor due to keeping their faith. Would they allow an Emperor to change their faith? Perhaps that was not the cause of Nero's persecutions. Christian resistance to becoming just another religion? In fact, if Christianity before 325 were indeed how Brown's characters and many modern neo-gnostics describe it, it would never have been persecuted since it would have fitted in perfectly with so many other pagan options. Christianity was always persecuted for not accepting the religious demands laid down by the political regime and for proclaiming that only Jesus Christ is God, along with the Father and the Holy Spirit.

A Host of Other Errors

SANDRA MIESEL, A CATHOLIC JOURNALIST specializing in modern popular literature, cannot help making a list of miscellaneous errors in the book, an example being its "impeccable" research.

According to her, "he (Dan Brown) claims that the motions of the planet Venus trace a pentacle, the so-called Ishtar pentagram, symbolizing the goddess—Ishtar is Astarte or Aphrodite. But it isn't a perfect figure and has nothing to do with the length of the Olympiad. The ancient Olympic games were celebrated in honour of Zeus Olympias, not the cycles of Venus Aphrodite, and occurred every four years.

"The novelist's contention that the five linked rings of the modern Olympic Games are a secret tribute to the goddess is also wrong— each set of games was supposed to add a ring to the design, but the organizers stopped at five.

"The novel presents a cathedral's long hollow nave as a secret tribute to a woman's womb...complete with receding labial ridges, etc... This is taken from the pseudohistory book *The Templar Revelation,* which asserted that the Knights Templar masterminded the design of cathedrals. Of course, this assertion is false: the Templars had nothing to do with the cathedrals of their time, which were commissioned by bishops and their canons. The cathedrals were either modelled on the Church of the Holy Sepulchre or Roman basilicas, rectangular civil buildings.

"The Priory is an actual organization officially registered with the French government in 1956, which most likely originated after World War II, although they defend themselves as heirs to the Freemasons, Templars, Egyptians, etc. The novel's list of Grand Masters—which include Leonardo da Vinci, Isaac Newton, and Victor Hugo—is not credible.

"Brown says that the tetragrammaton (YHWH), God in Hebrew letters, derives from 'Jehovah, an androgynous physical union between the masculine Jah and the pre-Hebraic name for Eve, Havah.' Apparently, nobody has explained to Brown that Jehovah is actually a 16th-century rendering of Yahweh using the vowels of Adonai.

"Tarot cards do not teach goddess doctrine. They were invented for innocent gaming purposes in the 15th century and didn't acquire occult associations until the late 18th. The notion of diamonds symbolizing pentacles is a deliberate misrepresentation by British occultist A. E. Waite. What would esoterics have to say about Spanish playing cards with the copas suits—female sex symbols—and the espadas suit—phallic symbols, perhaps similar to clubs...?

"Pope Clement V did not suppress the Templars in a Machiavellian plan, nor did he toss their ashes into the Tiber: the Tiber is in Rome, whereas Clement V was the first pope of Avignon. The initiative for crushing the Templars came from King Philip the Fair of France. Freemasons and even Nazis have longed to be heirs to Templars. Now it's the turn of neo-Gnostics. 'Mona Lisa' does not represent an androgynous person but Madonna Lisa, wife of Francesco di Bartolomeo del Giocondo. The name is not an anagram of two Egyptian deities, Amon and L'Isa (Italian for Isis).

"In Da Vinci's 'Last Supper,' there is no central chalice on the table and the young, handsome St. John, the beloved disciple, appears. The novel maintains that the handsome young man is in fact Mary Magdalene, that she is the Holy Grail. The truth is that the chalice is not represented because the painting is describing The Last Supper as it appears in St. John's Gospel, without the Institution of the Eucharist; more specifically when Jesus warns, 'One of you will betray me' (John 13:21).

"The novel claims that Leonardo received many commissions from the Church and 'hundreds of lucrative Vatican commissions.' Actually, Da Vinci spent very little time in the city and was hardly sent any commissions.

"In the book, Leonardo is depicted as an ostentatious homosexual. In fact, although during his youth he was accused of sodomy, his sexual leanings are not at all clear.

"The heroine, Sophie Neveu, uses Da Vinci's painting 'The Madonna of the Rocks' as a shield and presses it against her body so far that it bends. Quite astonishing given that it is a painting on wood, not canvas, and is almost two meters tall.

"The protagonists of the novel declare that 'during three hundred years of witch hunts, the church burned at the stake an astounding five million women.' This figure is repeated in neo-pagan, wicca, new age, and radical feminist literature, although other modern witch-craft websites and texts speak of about nine million women. Neo-pagans need their own Shoah. Reliable historical records show that between the years 1400 and 1800 in Europe, around 30,000 to 80,000 persons were executed as witches. Not all were burned, not all were women, and the majority were not executed by Church officials or even Catholics. Most of the victims were in Germany, coinciding with the peasant and Protestant revolts of the 16th and 17th centuries. When one region changed name, accusations of witchcraft and mass hysteria abounded. The civil, local, and municipal courts were especially enthusiastic, above all in Calvinist and Lutheran areas. In any case, witches have been persecuted and punished by death by the Egyptians, Greeks, Romans, and Vikings, among others. Paganism has always executed warlocks and witches. There are no historical foundations to support the feminist neo-pagan idea that witchcraft was a pre-Christian feminist religion.

"We could go on examining the false claims and deceits of this bestseller full of errors, not to mention its literary quality. But is a novel really worth so much effort? The answer has to be yes: for thousands of young persons and adults this will be their first and probably only introduction to the ancient history of the Church, a history spotted with the blood of martyrs and the ink of Evangelists, Apologists, Philosophers, and Fathers. It would not be fitting for the Christians of the 21st century to give over to neo-paganism that which the early Christians won with their steadfast fidelity to Jesus without a fight or with no answer."

AS YOU CAN SEE, THE RAGE IS OVERWHELMING and the arguments that contradict the fundamental points of this book apparently convincing. However, the reader should not forget that the main principle of journalism is being exercised here: inform rigorously, giving both sides of the argument. Indeed, the other, "pagan" side is not without equally convincing arguments. And this is not the only newspaper to give us a general idea of the criticism launched against the book, or rather to criticize it. Peter Millar tackled the thorny issue in the prestigious *Times* of London on June 21, 2003, under the suggestive title "Holy Humbug." His words were:

"There is something about archaeological quests, ancient religious relics, and mystical iconography that can turn the average bombs and bullets story into a real magical mystery tour.

"So a novel that begins with the bizarre murder of a Louvre curator, the successor to Leonardo da Vinci and Isaac Newton as the head of a secret society dedicated to concealing the Holy Grail and the truth about Christ, raises the hairs on the back of the neck and almost inspires faith in the publisher's hype.

"But the title of Dan Brown's *The Da Vinci Code* ought to be a warning, evoking the infamous formula of Robert Ludlum: definite article and ordinary word, with an exotic epithet interposed.

"From *The Scarlatti Inheritance* via *The Matarese Circle* to his final *The Prometheus Deception*, Ludlum turned out a string of extravagant plots acted out by cardboard characters uttering ludicrous dialogue.

"Dan Brown, I am afraid, is his worthy successor.

"This is without doubt the silliest, most inaccurate, ill-informed, stereotype-driven, cloth-eared, cardboard-cutout-populated piece of pulp fiction that I have read. And that's saying something.

"It would be bad enough that Brown has gone into New Age over-drive by trying to draw together the Grail, Mary Magdalene, the Knights Templar, the Priory of Sion, Rosicrucianism, Fibonacci numbers, the Isis cult, and the Age of Aquarius. But he has done it so sloppily. Early on there is a hint when Sophie, the French police cryptography expert heroine, reveals that her grandfather told her 'an astounding 92' other words could be made out of the English word 'planets.'

"'Sophie spent three days with an English dictionary until she found them all.'

"I am no cryptographer, but, including plurals, I managed to notch up 86 in 30 minutes.

"No surprise, then, when Sophie and her American symbologist companion are flummoxed by a strange written text that they suspect may be a form of ancient Semitic. It turns out to be longhand English mirror-writing (which is exactly what it looks like).

"These might be minor niggles were it not for the fact that the plot is essentially a treasure hunt involving precisely such clues. It takes them an unconscionably long time to figure out that her name is a form of 'sofia,' meaning 'wisdom.'

"Maybe that is not so strange after all. Apart from the 'puzzles,' the book is littered with misconceptions, howlers, and location descriptions that come straight out of tourist guide books.

"Brown obviously believes it is hard for French mobile phones to call 'transatlantic,' that Interpol records each night who is sleeping in which Paris hotel room, that someone in Scotland Yard answers the phone with 'This is the London police,' that English is a language that has no Latin roots, and England a country where it always rains (OK, so he may be right there).

"Inevitably, the dodgy British character is an upper-class Gielgudesque parody called Sir Leigh Teabing, whose test to let them through his security gates is to ask how they take their tea.

"The mystery's solution is wholly unsatisfactory and the assumed bad guys, Opus Dei and the Vatican, are let off the hook, presumably for fear of American lawsuits.

"Brown's publishers have drummed up a handful of glowing comments from American thriller writers just bubbling under the first division. I can only assume the reason for their fulsome praise was because this makes their own work look like masterpieces in comparison."

AND SO IT GOES ON. Spanish newspapers also followed suit, generally to level fierce criticism at a literary work that continued (and continues) to cause a great deal of controversy. The newspaper *El Mundo*, in its offprint *El Cultural*, ran the following report by Rafael Narbona on December 4, 2003: "Books that are born with the vocation of being a best-seller cannot hide the fact that they are manufactured goods. *The Da Vinci Code* is not a work of creation but an artifact designed to become a commercial hit. It contains all the elements for an easy success: a detective plot with political and religious links, stereotyped characters, doses of philosophical transcendence, eroticism without shrillness, and flat writing.

"Robert Langdon, an expert in symbols who resembles Harrison Ford, will discover that the Holy Grail is not a chalice but the secret name for Mary Magdalene. A descendent of kings, Mary Magdalene was not a prostitute but the wife of Jesus and mother of his daughter, Sarah. Her womb received the blood of Christ and her mission was to perpetuate the lineage of a mortal prophet who only became the Son of God due to later manipulations. Jesus chose Magdalene to lead the Church, but Rome never accepted this legacy and organized the Crusades to destroy the documents that hid the truth.

"The Priory of Sion was set up as a secret society assigned to preserve the proof of this bloodline lineage started by Jesus and Magdalene. Leonardo da Vinci, Botticelli, Newton, and Victor Hugo were members of this society. They fulfilled their pledge, but planted symbols in their work that alluded to the story: the apostle sitting to the right of Christ in 'The Last Supper' is none other than Mary Magdalene.

"Perhaps Brown is trying to emulate Umberto Eco by blending mystery, intellectualism, and philosophy, but he has only succeeded in writing an opportunistic and naive book. Langdon's perplexity over a written text that he attributes to a dead language is settled when it turns out to be mirror-writing. The Vatican's alleged involvement only reveals Brown's obscene delight in creating scandal. Ron Howard has already revealed his intention to adapt the book to the big screen. If it is true that bad books inspire excellent films, then we can expect a masterpiece."

AS WE WILL SEE LATER ON, the journalists of the Spanish newspaper were on the right track, but evidently it appeared that they had gotten the wrong end of the stick.

This introduction aims to show the impact of this famous book on the whole world, from Japan to Hawaii, from Chile to Finland. Of course, it would not be complete without the American press, some of which received Brown with fanatical devotion in one sense or another. On September 27, 2003, Thomas Roeser wrote the following for the *Chicago Sun Times*: "In our 'correct' society, a statement seen as racist, anti-Semitic, anti-woman, or gay bashing will disqualify a writer for years—but not insults to Jesus Christ and those who follow his precepts. Far from it: enlarge shop-worn Catholic-conspiracy tales into book length, and it can make you rich and famous, as it has one Dan Brown, author of *The Da Vinci Code*. The novel mixes fact with fiction in docudrama form, spewing a passel of baseless conjectures against Catholicism, representing modern feminist revisionist theory. The novel is part of a genre to present a hate-filled stereotype of Roman Catholicism as a villain. While hatred of Roman Catholicism dominates the book, no part of the church receives more invective than Opus Dei."

JUST DAYS EARLIER, the prestigious *New York Daily News* headed one of its reports "'Code' Hot, Critics Hotter," in which journalist Celia McGee went on to explain that "he (Brown) borrows heavily from two earlier works of amateur research, *The Templar Revelation: Secret Guardians of the True Identity of Christ* and *Holy Blood, Holy Grail*, a speculative look into Jesus' bloodline. Both have been discredited by most scholars. His glaring errors can only fail to catch the attention of poorly-educated readers..."

NEVERTHELESS, it cannot be said that *The New York Times* was more gracious when one of its most acclaimed critics, Bruce Boucher, pontificated about *The Da Vinci Code*: "Rather than film, however, there seems to an opera lurking in these pages, and Mr. Brown could do worse than weigh the immortal advice of Voltaire: '*If it's too silly to be said, it can always be sung.*'"

HARSH? There are a few other adjectives that could be used to describe the stark brutality with which some of the world's top media have vented their anger on this book. Let's look at a few more examples.

On June 8, 2003, *Our Sunday Visitor* encouraged its readers to take up a merciless fight against this novel, because the contents "are an attack on Catholicism." The author, Amy Welborn, did not avoid direct confrontation, declaring that "*The Da Vinci Code* is neither learned nor challenging, except to the reader's patience. Moreover, it's not even really suspenseful and the writing is shockingly banal, even for genre fiction. It's a pretentious, bigoted, tendentious mess. Hardly any of this background is original. Most of it is derived directly from the fantasy-disguised-as historical work *Holy Blood, Holy Grail*, and what is not is cobbled from other bits of well-worn and risible nuggets of esoteric and Gnostic conspiracy theories. Brown's treatment of the Roman Catholic Church is unoriginal as well, as he uncritically repeats, among many other lies and distortions, the canard that the Church was responsible for killing five million accused witches during the medieval period. It's not even the well-crafted suspense novel it's presented as. There is precious little action here."

AND SO THEY COME, ONE AFTER ANOTHER. What on earth does Brown's work contain to arouse so much fury among critics? No doubt something highly suggestive, or perhaps a little too uncomfortable.

Leaving behind the frenzied controversy and heated debates, and appealing to the freedom of journalists to present the results of their sometimes years-long research, we will try to produce some answers to so many questions.

At this point, readers who are not experts in these matters must not get bogged down with too many prejudices. If you identify yourself as one of those polemicists, then this book is not for you. On the other hand, if you want to learn another version of the story, the one not usually found in textbooks, then you have just made a good move.

The chronicles over the centuries are revealing enough to allow us to exercise a right as human as it is necessary—to doubt.

While avoiding biases and taking one "side" or the other, this book sums up a lifetime of travelling to places, some far away, that have been marked by the presence of an exceptional person that history has decided to name Jesus, and call Christ. The aim of these pages is to provide curious readers with the keys hidden in this best-seller of which almost ten million copies have been sold around the world and which has become a true publishing, and social, phenomenon. The author has cleverly wrapped up "apocryphal history" in a plot worthy of adventure novels. The only conclusion we can draw at this stage is that the past does interest; even more so, people get excited about that past, releasing the gods and devils that we all carry inside us. Could that be the key to the success of *The Da Vinci Code*? The perfect combination of fictitious elements with others, behind which many believe is hidden the true story of the past two thousand years; a story of secret conspiracies, of bloody battles to defend respective interests, some to protect the secret…and others to destroy it. That is what the pages of Dan Brown's polemic book contain. Of course, each person may make of it what they will. *Introit…*

LORENZO FERNÁNDEZ BUENO

ACT I

King Jesus

> *"...son of David, son of Abraham..."*
>
> (MATTHEW 1:1)

THE LAST TIME HE WAS SEEN He did not look very well. He had been nailed to a cross and terrible wounds oozed from His back, the result of a violent whipping; His hands were pierced at strategic points to avoid tearing the tendons in the area, and the nails must have caused unbearable shocks to His nervous system; His pelvis rubbed against the rough surface of the vertical trunk lacerating the perineum; the bones in His feet had shattered like glass due to the brutal stab of the nails that fastened Him to the dark wood and His lungs, far from being divine, struggled to draw in all the air they could, although He was barely able to grasp small amounts. He was, moreover, dehydrated, not having consumed food or drink for more than fifty hours, and He no longer looked anything like the man He used to be. Who was He, by the way?

We can imagine a drop of thick blood trickling down His body, just as though we were one of those people looking up in their role as silent witnesses. The drop of blood falls to the earth—plop!—hollowed out like a chalice for the occasion. And that drop of blood was an ever-lasting seed...

What do we believe we know?

"THERE ARE SO MANY OTHER THINGS THAT JESUS DID, which if they were written one by one, I suppose that even the world itself could not contain the books that would be written." That is how John the Evangelist finishes. But he—and all the other chroniclers—would have been wise to have been more meticulous in their details, because in that case the heading of this section would be: "What do we know?" The information is so vague—as you will see—and reporters so dreadful that many other authors have attempted to rewrite the story of the man they called Jesus of Nazareth. As a result, essays and novels have been written, some of which seem to have spiralled downwards into delirium. Is that the case of *The Da Vinci Code*, the novel by Dan Brown? Or does he perhaps get

it so right that millions of people have been captivated when reading it?

What we know about Jesus is taken from the four small books written by people who went by the names of Matthew, Mark, Luke, and John. These books, popularly known as Gospels—a word that used to refer to a messenger who brought news, either good or bad—ended up being the only ones accepted by the Church, as we will see later on, and went on to be bringers of "Good News." What did they consist of? Well, basically that God had sent His Son to Earth to preach a message, and then He had died to redeem our sins. This was because in Jewish culture it had been decided that man had sinned at the beginning, when Eve made the grave error of eating the forbidden fruit in the Garden of Eden. But how can we be so sure that the version that those chroniclers gave us is the right one? We can never really know for sure. Only the walking stick of faith can aid us along that path; faith in the Church's opinion, we mean.

Adam and Eve, responsible for "sinful" humanity.

Matthew, who came to be represented in religious iconography on Romanesque façades as an angel, may have been the tax collector who, according to the Gospel, Jesus included among His followers while hardly saying a word to him. Eusebio wrote that he preached for fifteen years in Judea before taking his Gospel to Ethiopia. Tradition has it that he is buried in Salerno, Italy. The exegetes claim that he used Mark, as well as an alleged unknown source containing Jesus' sayings, for his work. All of this may have been written circa 80 AD, that is, half a century after what he claims to relate faithfully actually happened.

The Gospel according to Mark—the lion in Romanesque illustrations of the four Evangelists representing a four-headed God—prefers to describe what happened to Jesus and His followers in Jerusalem over a few days, and dedicates a third of his book to this. On the contrary, the rest of His life only takes up a fourth of the book. When was it written? It is said that it could have been between 65 and 70 AD, which means that he may have been trying to deliver a message of hope to the Christians who were being tortured by Rome around that time. Whatever the case, he did not include any details until at least thirty years after those spectacular events had taken place.

As for Luke—the bull of the four Evangelists—we can say that he was an educated and learned man, maybe a physician and native of Assyria, and that he was the assistant of a subject known as Saul, persecutor of Christians before becoming His most fervent follower and being renamed Paul (you have probably heard of Paul of Tarsus). Luke is his spokesperson. He is also the author of The Acts of the Apostles—which we will study in greater depth further on—which are both dedicated to Theophilus, although we do not know whether the latter is a case of literary license—"friend of God?"—or a real person. The text may have been written circa 80 AD.

Finally, there are the manuscripts ascribed to John, who is usually said to be no other than Zebedee, "the Son of Thunder," brother of James and one of the persons who always seems to be close to Jesus in these stories. However, it would seem outlandish to claim that an uneducated fisherman was able to compose such a dark text full of symbols and with the most different writing style from the rest. The latter are called synoptic—from the Greek *syn-orao*: to see as a whole— since when they are set out in a column, the events can be followed more or less in order. However, John strays from this column and produces a text that we could consider to be enlightening and which experts claim may have been written around 100 AD.

Representation of the Four Evangelists in the Church of Santiago, in the town of Carrión de los Condes, Castile-Leon.

For centuries the Church has endeavored to fabricate a Jesus to meet its desires, which are basically those of Paul of Tarsus who is lauded and praised time and again in the Acts until he is known as the Apostle to the Gentiles. In spite of the title of this text—The Acts of the Apostles—only Peter, John, and James are mentioned in passing, with no sign of the rest. The only protagonist is Paul, time and time again. Paul, who boasts about not knowing Jesus' direct disciples no less than three years after joining the Christian religion. Paul, who holds a different Christian theory violently opposed to the rest of Jesus' followers, as stated in the book *The Hidden "Lives" of Jesus* (Ed. Nowtilus, 2002). Paul, who maybe made a man—although extraordinary—into a God.

In 1947, in Qumran next to the Dead Sea, a chance discovery was made, the importance of which is yet to be fully gauged. A Bedouin group stumbled upon a hoard of texts that are generally known as the Dead Sea Scrolls, the contents of which are still the topic of debates, since some researchers claim that they provide valuable background for understanding the origins of the Christian movement. These scrolls could be the legacy of one of the three most powerful Jewish sects that existed in Palestine in the time of Jesus: the Essenes. Then there are those who declare that this was where Jesus learned all that He practiced, and even those who portray Him as nationalist, violently opposed to the Roman oppression.

Two years earlier in 1945, in Nag Hammadi, Upper Egypt, another discovery was made, again by chance—is chance the pseudonym for God?—of an authentic collection of texts that have been called "Gnostic." These once again give an image of Jesus completely at odds with that provided by the four Evangelists.

It so happened that no sooner had our protagonist died than some people wanted to stir up a hornet's nest and harm the interests of Paul, who had demonstrated astonishing "commercial" skills in presenting the Christian "product" to a far-reaching "market." Let us explain: the Greco-Roman world was bursting with Gods. One more would not have changed the divine census. However, the amazing thing about this God was that He had been a man, during whose life many extraordinary events had occurred, not least having been born to a Virgin and, lo and behold, having risen again on the third day. This was Paul's "product." The very same that brought him into conflict with Jesus' followers who did know the Master, which is something Paul of Tarsus could not say.

This was why he tried to make up for his disadvantage by seeing a direct heavenly vision, being literally knocked off his high horse into the bargain.

Nonetheless, there were many Christians who did not agree with that version and recorded what they knew. Later, during the 2nd and 3rd centuries, many *Apocryphal* Gospels began to circulate out of control. These included ideas taken from sun-worshipping religions, especially Egyptian, as you will later see.

The Dead Sea Scrolls revealed a great deal...

But with the passing of time, following Constantine's vision of the cross in the sky with the words "In hoc signo vinces" (*in this sign thou shalt conquer*), the Church went from being tortured to torturer. In 313, Emperor Constantine proclaimed the Edict of Milan, which established the freedom of this religion before he became a militant Christian himself. Under his mandate the Council of Nicea was called in 325 AD, at which, *inter alia*, all the Christian texts that the Pauline Church did not like were destroyed. Why?

Among other things, the Gnostic texts spoke of the possibility that mankind would come into contact with God without the mediation of any clergy. They claimed the existence of a secret doctrine taught by Jesus to a group of followers who were not the so-called Apostles and which, when applied, would bring *gnosis* or "knowledge." According to Elaine Pagels, by achieving gnosis man—or woman, since that was the other key question— *"becomes no longer a Christian, but a Christ."* These mysterious words spoken by Jesus may have been written down somewhere. For this reason, Irenaeus, bishop of Lyon in 180 AD and militant in the Church's "official" group, stated *"heretics boast that they have many more gospels than there really are."*

But we mentioned women.

Precisely. In these mysterious teachings that Jesus apparently gave to a group of chosen ones, women played a special role. They could officiate at ceremonies, and in fact there were groups such as the *ophites*— from *ofis*, the Greek for serpent—who worshipped the serpent as the Bestower of Knowledge and the one who opened Eve's eyes. Afterwards, Eve became Adam's master. Not too much for an untrained clerical stomach to swallow!

In Dan Brown's novel, one of the characters, Teabing, sums up the above for Sophie, which we can narrow down by choosing just a sample of quotes from this scene. For instance, the British historian maintains that: *"as a descendant of the lines of King Solomon and King David, Jesus possessed a rightful claim to the throne of the King of the Jews,"* and goes on to add: *"Understandably, His life was recorded by thousands of followers across the land (…). More than eighty gospels were considered for the New Testament, and yet only a relative few were chosen for inclusion—Matthew, Mark, Luke, and John among them."*

Regarding Constantine's political and religious stance that we have briefly described, the author of *The Da Vinci Code* alludes to the Emperor's skill as a "businessman." Seeing that Christianity was going from strength to strength, he fused pagan symbols onto the new Christian orthodoxy. Langdon, another of the main characters in the novel, tells Sophie: *"The vestiges of pagan religion in Christian symbology are undeniable. Egyptian sun disks became the halos of Catholic saints."* Later Teabing declares: *"Nothing in Christianity is original."* The novelist then goes on to state: *"Originally (...) Christians honored the Jewish Sabbath of Saturday, but Constantine shifted it to coincide with the pagan's veneration day of the sun."* He also maintains that they looked for dates for the birth of Jesus for centuries, until in the end they obliged people to celebrate the event on the winter solstice when the new sun is "born."

Brown also quotes Napoleon, who stated *"What is history but a fable agreed upon?"* with regard to the documents that have reached us today due to the Church's zeal, and many others that have not reached us for the exact same reason. It is clear that the Pauline Church was the one to succeed. This highly successful novel is largely based on the possible existence of the "Purist Documents" which are *"thousands of pages of unaltered, pre-Constantine documents, written by the early followers of Jesus, revering Him as a wholly human teacher and prophet. Also rumored to be part of the treasure is the legendary 'Q' Document—a manuscript that even the Vatican admits they believe exists. Allegedly, it is a book of Jesus' teachings, possibly written in His own hand."*

The book skilfully combines literary plots with true stories, as we have explained up until now. And these damned texts existed, as did their authors. All of them were destroyed by the official Church. Not one survived to tell the story. Or did they?

The urgent need for a Savior

IF WE HAD TO make a chronological summary of what happened to the Jewish people from when Abraham grew a long beard and left Ur of the Chaldees to wander into all sorts of difficulties ordered by his whimsical and warlike God, the result would be something like the following:

Abraham began his unusual adventure around 1800 BC. Later came his most popular descendants: Isaac, Jacob—later called Israel—and

9

the twelve sons of the latter, all of whom ended up in Egypt circa 1650 BC. They stayed there until Moses took them out of the country around 1250, probably after having stolen secret knowledge from the priests of the Nile.

David, King of Israel and the first of a divine lineage.

After forty years of tanning under the harsh desert sun, fighting with each other and with everyone else, they decided to settle in the so-called "Promised Land," home to other people, all of whom suffered the wrath of Jehovah, the God of the Old Testament.

Moses died and was succeeded by Joshua, but it was not until the arrival of Saul that the monarchy was inaugurated in this land. The second king was called David, who is of interest to us at this stage. He was conqueror of the capital of the Jebusites, Jerusalem. His government lasted from 1012 to 972 BC. Later came the famous and enigmatic Solomon, who built the First Temple to hide the Ark of the Covenant that Jehovah had ordered Moses to build in the desert.

Why are we interested in David? Because, if we choose to believe the "official" Gospels, Jesus is a descendant of his lineage. Let us look at some more history.

After Solomon, the kingdom was divided into Israel to the north and Judea to the south. This was the prelude to a tragedy. In 586, King Nebuchadnezzar took Jerusalem and the Jews were deported to Babylon. And so the captivity began, until Cyrus the Persian issued an edict for the Jews to return to Jerusalem in 538 BC and a second temple was built. Next came the conquest by Alexander the Great in 332 BC, and several further upheavals until Pompey took possession of the land in 63 BC and included it in the impressive Roman Empire. By then, and in view of the hard times they had gone through, the idea of a Savior, a liberator in this "stubborn" land, had taken off.

Before we go on, let us look at some ideas put forward by authors like Laurence Gardner about wise King Solomon's permissiveness with regard to the worship of other Gods—especially a Goddess—of the people who lived in the conquered lands (I-Kings 11:4-10). This feminine deity was called Asherah (in Egypt we would have come across her under the name of Isis). This source maintains that the Jewish idea of a male king was not conceived until the captivity in Babylon, given that it was there, and nowhere else, that most of the books that later constituted the Bible were compiled. This explains why clearly Sumerian and Mesopotamian stories have been woven in, such as the Tower of Babel, the Garden of Eden, and the Flood. It was also there, in the cold captivity, that the idea of a Savior was born, an anointed King, a political leader.

Earlier, Isaiah—who we can tentatively place at 700 BC—seeing the threat from Assyria came up with a song for the hope of the people and to threaten King Ahaz: *"Hear then, O house of David (...) Therefore the Lord himself will give you a sign. Behold, a virgin shall conceive and bear a son, and shall call his name Emmanuel."* Supposedly, Ahaz would have been somewhat alarmed. But if he were to be told that the infant was to be born seven hundred years later, he would have rolled around laughing. So did that threat really allude to Jesus, who was obviously not called Emmanuel by the way?

Was the prophecy fulfilled?

When Jesus came into the world, Rome was the owner and lord of Palestine. The Jews loathed the invaders and a leader would have put the Empire in danger. A true Savior, with the appropriate religious flavor, was also unacceptable for the priests of the Sanhedrin. We are even tempted to say that for the Sanhedrin, teeming with Pharisees and Sadducees, that Savior was as detrimental as the real Jesus would be to the Church today.

The three synoptic Gospels strive to emphasize the real genealogy of Jesus. Matthew starts by writing: *"...son of David, son of Abraham,"* (Matthew, 1:1). Several verses on, he stresses the miraculous conception of Jesus and, without giving us respite, turns to Micah's prophecy (5:2) to justify the adoration of the Magi: *"But thou, Bethlehem Ephratah, though thou be little among the thousands of Judah, yet out of thee shall he come forth unto me that is to be ruler in Israel."* Note the word "ruler."

There is also Isaiah's prophecy (9:1): *"Land of Zebulun and land of Naphtali (...) the people living in darkness have seen a great light..."*

Mark and Luke pay attention to another remarkable man, a *"voice of one calling in the desert."* Of course, we are referring to John, then known as "the Baptist." He appears as a relative of Jesus, since his Mother, Elizabeth, was Mary's cousin. John comes before Jesus in everything: he was born first, a "strange phenomenon;" his mother had not been able to have children until Jehovah worked one of his miracles, not without first rendering his father, Zechariah, mute until the birth of the child. He was also the first to achieve fame and importance in the community, and even some of the disciples that later became Jesus' servers were his; for example Andrew, brother of Peter.

So why all the interest in John? Some authors, such as Picknett and Price, suggest that Jesus was a usurper, an impostor who snatched leadership away from John. They maintain that there are still followers of John the Baptist's Church today, and that this may have been the religious model that the Knights Templar discovered in the Holy Land. This would have prompted their supposed rejection of the symbol of Jesus.

In our opinion, *The Da Vinci Code* skims over this issue, without developing it later in the plot. It happens when Sophie senses that her grandfather, Jacques Saunière, might have left her a last legacy behind Da Vinci's "Madonna of the Rocks." This canvas painting shows the Virgin Mary in the center with Jesus as an infant child on her right, and on her left the angel Uriel and John the Baptist, also a child. In their book *The Templar Revelation*, Picknett and Price echo what we are about to sum up, the same poorly-developed issue we come across in the novel.

What really jumps out at us in this scene is that it is not Jesus who is blessing John, as would be logical, but John is blessing Jesus, as though he is the superior authority. Furthermore, Mary is holding one hand up towards John, which these authors, and we quote from the novel, interpret as *"a decidedly threatening gesture."* Also, the angel Uriel is below Mary, which Brown reads—and presents through the character in the novel, Langdon—as follows: *"...Just below Mary's curled fingers, Uriel was making a cutting gesture with his hand—as if slicing the neck of the invisible head gripped by Mary's claw-like hand."*

These bold interpretations are not the only ones that have been made on all these issues: Here is another.

To understand the following, it is necessary to shake off the idea that Mary was a virgin when she gave birth and that she remained so. The Gospels clearly state that Jesus had more brothers: James, Joseph, Simon, and Judas (Matthew, 13:55; Mark 3:32; Acts 1:14). The question Gardner asks himself out loud is whether, seeing as Jesus was the firstborn and was descendant of the line of King David as the Gospels emphasize, He would have had the right to hold that position if He had been born outside marital orthodoxy? He goes on to expound a curious theory: in his opinion, Jesus was a political ruler with royal blood who was leader of the sect of the Nazarenes. The name "Nazarene" should not be translated as "from Nazareth" according to this theory. This is the same sect of which, as appears in Acts (24:5), Paul became leader later of. John the Baptist was also a member of this sect, which may have absorbed the philosophy of the Essenes. Of course, another member was James, the brother of Jesus, who *had* been born in an "orthodox" manner in the family. According to Gardner, the dilemma was deciding who had the right to be leader of the sect: Jesus, the eldest but "anomalously" born, or James.

It was to elucidate this point, says this source, that Jesus' parents took him to the temple. They wanted to hear the verdict of Rabbi Simon (Luke 2:25-35). The author continues by saying that when James was born, however, the faction split. The Hellenised Jews considered Jesus to be the Lord's Anointed or *Khristos*, while the Orthodox Jews chose James. The latter received the support of Sadoc the priest, who was none other than John the Baptist. This helps to explain to other researchers the reason why Jesus did not move a muscle to help the Baptist when the latter fell at the hands of Herod.

Now that we mention Herod, let us look at Robert Ambelain's examination of a curious fact that appears in Luke (13:31). This is the warning that some Pharisees gave Jesus, when supposedly He had scarcely begun his public life, that the King wanted to kill Him. Jesus angrily responds: *"Go tell that fox (...)."* Ambelain examines the reasons that Herod would have to kill a man who had not yet done anything out of the ordinary. The answer might be that he knew that that man was a descendant of the House of David, the true owner of the crown that the Romans had given Herod permission to wear on his head.

Once He was ready to begin His "pastoral" activity, according to the Catholic version, or political version according to other suggestions, Jesus was surrounded by a group of followers. There is something mysterious about the choice of these followers, at least the *notables* that the Gospels quoted. It cannot be denied that it is strange that someone who says: *"And ye shall be hated of all for my name's sake"* (Matthew 10:22), finds followers just by making them the outlandish proposal of turning them into *"fishers of people."* And that they immediately leave their families and possessions. Odd, don't you think?

Gardner quite rightly points out that *"Jesus' plans were unknown and he had still not acquired a reputation for being Divine at that time. Therefore, it is clear that there is something missing in the Gospels."* We agree. But what is missing? Maybe we really are dealing with a divine being whose only purpose was to convince the people? If this is the case, why did He not convince everybody? Or perhaps His ministry had already begun and

**Al-Aqsa, in Jerusalem, on the site of the ruins of
King Solomon's Temple.**

He was a famous man when He appeared before His supposed future disciples? Or was it that they knew about Jesus' noble birth, since He was not a humble carpenter but a rabbi educated in the most mysterious sciences? If so, where did He receive His education? Gardner believes that the Gospels were written in metaphor and that they were highly politically charged, which is evident at times in Jesus' sayings, but which harm our traditional image of Him. The following are two examples: *"Think not that I am come to send peace on earth: I came not to send peace, but a sword"* (Matthew 10:34); *"...and he that hath no sword, let him sell his garment, and buy one"* (Luke 22:36). Except that almost all the so-called apostles must have had a sword already. What was the point if the movement was purely spiritual?

It is also difficult to fit these ideas in with Jesus' proposals to love thy neighbor or to turn the other cheek. Do you make anything of it? Or do we not have ears to hear and eyes to see? Was He talking in two different ways? Did He explain his true doctrine to a chosen few and not to those who appeared as disciples? Or were there two Jesuses? So many questions and so few answers! However, we will try to find some possible solutions to these enigmas.

Since we are dealing with the Apostles, we should mention some of the confusion that is created in this regard. John states that Andrew, brother of Peter, was one of John the Baptist's followers. The other three Evangelists only recount how Jesus proposes to turn a few into *"fishers of people,"* or how mysteriously Matthew the publican's calling took place. And so we have Peter, Andrew, John, James, Zebedee, and the aforementioned Matthew. Soon the list grows longer with Phillip and Bartholomew, Thomas, James of Alphaeus and Thaddaeus, Simon the Zealot and Judas Iscariot. These appear in the Gospel According to Matthew. But Mark's Gospel refers to Levi of Alphaeus, later adding Matthew's name. Levi also appears in Luke's narration (5:27), although here we find out more highly interesting information since he states that *"of them he chose twelve,"* referring to His disciples (Luke 6:13). Later there were more. How many more? The same Gospel says: *"the Lord chose another seventy-two"* (Luke 10:1). For his part, John mentions Nathaneal, which clearly creates a certain amount of confusion.

Were so many disciples really necessary for a spiritual mission? Was there one group that was the military arm and another that was the repository of an entirely different teaching?

Let us look at one last example of this confusion, which has also sparked all kinds of speculations: the case of the "Simons."

There is an army of people who go by the name of Simon. There is Simon "the Leper" who, it appears, lives in Bethany, our favorite town (as we shall soon explain). Ambelain is of the opinion that it is in his house that the mythical unction of Christ took place. Then there is Simon who it is alleged is called Peter. However, it turns out that another Simon is quoted as one of Jesus' brothers. Could it be the person who is later called Peter? Is it another person? Yes, it must be another person. We also have Simon "the Zealot," who was apparently armed to the teeth, as you would

Saint Peter, in a "Vision" by El Greco.

expect of a nationalist opposed to Rome. What was he doing in a group of mystics?

Nevertheless, Simon called Peter also draws a sword when Jesus is about to be seized. Are Simon Peter and Simon "the Zealot" one and the same? No, they cannot be, although some people think so. And all of the above must be different from Simon "the Cananaean" quoted by Mark (3:18), and from Simon Iscariot, allegedly father of Judas, according to John's Gospel (6:71).

Let us leave it there. This is only the beginning of the confusion.

We will now look at the fulfillment of the King's prophecy. Jesus' group decides to ride into Jerusalem during that memorable Easter—or was it not Easter?—and fulfil the prophecy that spoke of the Messiah. But you will remember that the people were expecting a liberator with a strong military arm. Have we not seen a warlike image of Jesus and a group of more than seventy loved—and armed—disciples?

Matthew recalls the words of Zechariah (9:9): *"Tell ye the daughter of Zion, Behold, thy King cometh unto thee, meek, and riding upon an ass..."* This shows that Jesus had a chain of followers capable of setting the scene for the prophecy to be fulfilled, even if in the Gospel he tries to miraculously explain what happened afterwards.

Mark writes (11:1): *"And when they came nigh to Jerusalem, unto Bethphage and Bethany, at the Mount of Olives, he sendeth forth two of his disciples and saith unto them, Go your way into the village over against you: and as soon as ye be entered into it, ye shall find a colt tied."* And that is how it happened. Jesus strove to fulfil the prophecy that spoke of a "king" from the House of David. It is all set so that all sides are mobilized and the people acclaim Him, and to start with it seems that this is going to happen. But something goes wrong; that is, if the real goal was a political one.

Jesus preaches and arrives at the temple where he expels the merchants and the money changers. He creates a scene but does not earn the support of the people. In the Gospel according to John: *"And though he had done so many signs in their presence, they believed not in him."* Why? Furthermore, *"and the chief priests and the scribes sought how they might take him by craft, and put him to death"* (Mark 14:1).

Gardner explains this situation by claiming that *"His compatriots did not share his dreams of unifying the people, including the Jews and gentiles, and fighting against Rome."* Is this a sufficient explanation? Who knows...? The notion we have is that something is still amiss in this whole affair. Indeed, we should take this opportunity to warn the reader that there is more confusion just around the corner.

Another teaching, other disciples

EARLIER, WE ASKED OURSELVES THE RHETORICAL QUESTION whether Jesus may have taught another doctrine to some of His followers who were perhaps not the well-known Apostles. And if so, we asked, where could He have learned whatever He taught?

In a way, we provided the answer to this when we said that since the times of Constantine—and probably much earlier too—Christianity had adapted some elements of Pagan, especially Egyptian, worship to its own advantage. Indeed, as we see it, Jesus was a true initiate of Egyptian mysteries, which He could have learned perfectly during His stay in the country of the Nile. This trip was even mentioned by Matthew: *"When he arose, he took the young child and his mother by night, and departed into Egypt: And was there until the death of Herod: that it might be fulfilled which was spoken of the Lord by the prophet, saying, Out of Egypt have I called my son"* (Matthew 2:14-15).

Thus, Jesus travelled to Egypt. This country, especially the city of Alexandria, was full of Jews. They numbered in the thousands; therefore it is highly possible that He immersed Himself in the religious and magic knowledge of the mystical rabbinical tradition: Kabbala.

On several occasions we have stressed the importance acquired by the city of Heliopolis, where mystical sun-worshipping took place. According to legend it was the resting ground of the "Ben-Ben" stone, the center of creation and the site where the Phoenix bird re-emerged from its ashes, an image synonymous with resurrection. In other words, in Heliopolis there was a great deal of knowledge about those words that would come to be constantly on Jesus' lips: life and resurrection.

It is impossible to sum up all the aspects of Jesus' doctrine that can be traced in ancient texts, inscriptions, and Egyptian religious customs. However, perhaps the most important aspect is what we have mentioned regarding the game of life and the possibility of resurrection, which the Pharaohs acted out in the famous *Heb Seb* festivals, held thirty years after the start of their reign. Part of these was a public ceremony—the rest, the most interesting part, being private. It would seem that as the result of a kind of ritual in which certain drugs or a "magic touch" may have played a part, the Pharaoh entered a state of lethargy similar to death, and then returned stronger, more valiant, and perhaps more just, or at least that is what they had the people believe. This was a temporary state borrowed from the ancient tradition of Osiris, a God who was betrayed by his brother Seth, his body dismembered and cast into oblivion; at least that is what it seemed. However, the legend goes on to reveal Osiris as raised from the dead on the third day through the mediation of his sister and wife Isis. We will return to this story later on, but now we will use it to introduce Jesus' relationship with Egypt, and to guess what resemblance there is between this entire episode and His death and Resurrection.

Moreover, with regard to the need to be just to enter the Heavenly Kingdom, we cannot elude the comparison between that heaven and the Egyptian kingdom of Maat, the Goddess of Justice, on whom all the subjects of the land of Pharaohs had to model their behavior.

Ambelain shows he agrees with us when he writes: *"It is more likely that it was in the heart of the Jewish community of Alexandria, that is, effectively in Egypt, where He received from the Jewish Kabbalists His initiation into the supreme mysteries of their secret cult,"* although he does not think it has anything to do with Egyptian tradition. This is because he has not noticed that this mastery of the secrets of numbers and words was what Moses learned in Egypt a long while beforehand; therefore it was not something with which the priests of the Nile were unfamiliar.

Up to this point, we have presented the possibility of a King Jesus, as He appears in the novel *The Da Vinci Code*. However, we have just brought into play an initiated Jesus, a priest and expert on the hidden secrets of Tradition. Is this all a blatant contradiction? We sincerely think not. In fact, this reinforces our "Egyptian proposal." Was a Pharaoh not a religious and political lord? From whom did Jesus' forefather Solomon draw inspiration in his kingdom but from the Pharaoh? Could Jesus not follow that same example? Was synarchy not the political model that the Templars of the Middle Ages wanted to put into practice? And finally, does this idea not justify the possibility of a military and political arm among Jesus' followers, and another repository of the secretive and mystic teaching?

Perhaps we can find an explanation in the following, which has given us a lot to think about: *"And with many such parables spake he the word unto them, as they were able to hear it. But without a parable spake he not unto them: and when they were alone, he expounded all things to his disciples"* (Mark 4:33).

But what were "all the things" that He explained to His "disciples" alone? Are these the Apostles? We are afraid not. And, if we are right, who were among the disciples? To answer this question we are faced with two options: turn to the banned Gospels or look through different eyes at the only Gospel that everyone agrees is the most esoteric and obscure of the four: the Gospel according to John. It is on these pages where we find our favorite Gospel characters, as well as the village involved in the mystery: Bethany.

It is this John who mentions a Nicodemus (John 3:1), *"ruler of the Jews;"* in other words, an important man in the community and probably a rabbi. With Nicodemus Jesus has one of his most revealing conversations about the initiation, although it is disguised in the text under the apparent impossibility of *"How can a man be born when he is old? Can he enter the second time into his mother's womb, and be born?"* Jesus of Nazareth answers, *"Ye must be born again,"* and is surprised that Nicodemus does not know this: *"Art thou a master of Israel, and knowest not these things?"* In other words, the logical thing would be for a rabbi to know this, since any true initiate would have "died" and been "born" into a new life. Of course, we are talking about Jesus. This is the old well-known lesson of initiation in Egypt.

Just in case this is not clear, one other character makes an appearance who we are also going to study: Lazarus, who had a firsthand initiation experience: a "death," a rite inside the Mother Earth, and a "resurrection." This process, like any initiation process, was a lengthy one, and so Jesus did not give in to the messages begging for help that reached him from Bethany. Lazarus had to pass the test on his own.

There are other curious people linked to the village of Bethany, such as Simon the Leper, Martha, and Mary—Oh, Mary! It seems to be Jesus' "headquarters" where many events take place, all of which are recounted by John, the most secretive Evangelist. The latter also mentions the special role that Joseph of Arimathea plays during Jesus' final moments, which we will deal with over the next few pages. For the time being, let us take a break in Bethany before continuing onwards to Jerusalem, as indeed Jesus used to do...

In the following chapter we will rescue from oblivion the rest of the "disciples" to whom Jesus "expounded all things" when they were alone.

The Dome of the Rock, a sacred site for the three religions.

Four days of confusion

FROM HERE ON, we need you to open your mind even further, if you can. We will ask you to read at your leisure some of the passages with which the Gospels intended—although this was really the Church's intention—to tell the events of the last four days of Jesus' life.

As far as we are concerned, they are all a big confusion. Let us see why.

The following is a summary of what supposedly happened:

—Thursday, April 6: Last Supper, at dusk, and Jesus' arrest, at nightfall, on the Mount of Olives.

—Friday, April 7: Jesus is tried, during the night; crucifixion and death.

—Saturday, April 8: Jesus is buried.

—Sunday, April 9: Resurrection—at daybreak.

The first mix-up is when all of this occurred. The first three Gospels agree that Jesus celebrated Passover before his death. John, on the other hand, writes *"before the feast of the Passover..."* (John 13:1), and also includes a rite not mentioned by the others, "washing the disciples' feet." This appears to be an act of initiation, which the ignorant apostles do not understand, least of all Peter.

The date on which the drama unfolds is therefore hazy. Yet there is more to come.

According to the Synoptic Gospels, the Last Supper supposedly took place on the night before the crucifixion, but none of the texts emphasize that this was a unique, new rite for them. This type of banquet is pointed out in the Essenic texts found at Qumran and it appears to be customary in Jesus' circles. Apart from the confusion over the dates and times, according to the aforementioned chronology, as Ambelain points out, it seems that the beginning of the end was on a Friday, the day of Venus or woman; the feminine " V " to which the novel *The Da Vinci Code* refers—while the Resurrection took place on a Sunday, the day of the

23

Sun or the masculine. This was another of the Church's victories, putting the masculine principle before the feminine.

Authors like Ambelain are especially surprised that Jewish priests would have negotiated Jesus' arrest with Rome at Passover, when supposedly Jerusalem was overflowing with visitors. Even Mark (14:2) and Matthew (26:5) quote the priests saying: *"Not on the feast [day], lest there be an uproar of the people..."* Moreover, if a public lesson were the aim of Jesus' death, it would hardly be achieved at Passover when all labor was banned: *"ye shall do no manner of servile work therein"* (Numbers 28:18).

The aforementioned author is surprised that Jesus was tried throughout the night, since according to Jewish Law no trials took place during those hours: *"darkness confuses the trial of man."* Regarding the Passover Supper, the Book of Exodus (12:22) also states *"And none of you shall go out at the door of his house until the morning."* This does not explain how after the supposed Passover Supper Jesus and His followers went to the Mount of Olives, when it must not have been easy to move around Jerusalem without the Roman guards stopping them, especially since they were a large group of agitators. A very large group at that, since no less than a cohort was sent to arrest Jesus, that is, six hundred elite soldiers plus the officers of the Sanhedrin: *"Judas then, having received a band [of men] and officers from the chief priests and Pharisees, cometh thither with lanterns and torches and weapons"* (John 18:3). Later on he stresses: *"Then the band and the captain and officers of the Jews took Jesus, and bound him"* (John 18:12).

It is evident that there are several anomalies throughout this scene. Why were so many soldiers necessary against only twelve men? The only explanation is that Jesus, as a political and religious leader, had a large number of troops at his disposal, who He told to sell their garments to buy swords. Yet, when Peter draws his sword and cuts off the ear of a servant called Malchus, Jesus reprimands him. Again, a blatant contradiction between the peacemaker and the Jesus who tells his people to bring a sword.

There are more confused events yet to come.

The author of the book *Jesus and the Mortal Secret of the Templars* expresses surprise at the fact that, even though Pontius Pilate sent his troops to arrest Jesus, the defendant is taken first to the house of Annas—*"And led him away to Annas first…"* (John 18:13)—and not to the representatives of Rome. In addition, it appears that He is being tried for blasphemy. What blasphemy? Saying that He was the Son of God? Why would that matter to Rome? Rome was more concerned about His being proclaimed King of Jews, which was what Pontius Pilate ordered written and placed on His cross: *"Jesus of Nazareth, King of Jews."* And, since the chief priests were not keen on the idea, he declared: *"What I have written I have written"* (John 19:22). And what can we say about the "correspondents'" confusion over the time of the crucifixion?

The "Golgotha" is a Christian symbol of the Crucifixion, as related in the Gospel. But there may be more to it…

Mark (15:25) claims He was crucified at the third hour, and that at the sixth hour a heavy darkness gathered over Jerusalem. On the other hand, John (19:14) tells us He was crucified at the sixth hour. This is not trivial, since depending on when He was crucified and when He died, a series of events could have taken place, as we will describe briefly below, which have resulted in a great deal of speculation.

It is well known that the Hebrew custom of keeping the Sabbath meant that many activities were prohibited once the sun had set on Friday, generally all those that involved labor. For instance, taking a body down from a cross, washing it, anointing it, and wrapping it in a shroud before burying it. Hence the haste with which one of Jesus' mysterious "disciples," Joseph of Arimathea, worked in view of the authorities. Or was all this haste not due to that reason?

Nevertheless, before His death, Jesus cried out to the heavens with a phrase that has sparked controversy: *"Eli, Eli, lama azavtani...,"* which has been translated as *"My God, my God, why hast Thou forsaken me?"* However, what the reader might not know is that these words are precisely the second verse of Psalm 22, entitled *"For the leader; according to 'The deer of the dawn'. A psalm of David."* This has prompted some researchers to wonder why a man undergoing dreadful suffering would remember the verse of a song. Of course, this man was not like any other. Yet, some people, such as the aforementioned Robert Ambelain, claim that Jesus did not recite a verse to the heavens, but that He actually shouted out powerful words of a magic formula. Ambelain boldly claims that this formula was: *"'Eli! ElOim! Lama Astagna Tani...,'* meaning 'Conspiracies! Curses! By Lama, Astagna, Tani,...'"* Lama and Astagna are names of *"spirits that rule the Western region of the world,"* while Tani would be *"one of the twelve names of the Spirits that rule the twelve hours of the day..."*

What does the reader prefer to believe? As for us, we are incredibly confused. And it is not even over yet.

Before this chilling cry, vinegar is offered to Jesus. How bizarre? Who could have been carrying a jar containing vinegar? Or was it usual to carry it to ease the suffering of those facing execution? There are all sorts of opinions on the matter. However, John clearly states that it was already prepared: *"Now there was set a vessel full of vinegar"* (John 19:29). Gardner offers the theory that the contents that Matthew (27:34) claims were wine mixed with honey, were *"wine mixed with snake poison,"* a mixture that, carefully prepared, could cause *"unconsciousness or death."*

The theory that he puts forwards, and which others corroborate, is that a meticulous plan was hatched in which Jesus appeared to be dead but was not. Joseph of Arimathea, who was fully involved in the affair, pulled all the strings so that they could take down the accused as soon as possible, and they did not even break His legs, which was the common practice. They called Pilate and told him that Jesus was dead. The Roman was surprised that it was over so quickly: *"And Pilate marvelled if he were already dead"* (Mark 15:44). Joseph of Arimathea appealed to the Governor until he granted permission to take down the dead body and bring it to a tomb they had prepared. All this was done with great speed. Was it because they were in a hurry in view of the imminent Sabbath? Or was it already the Sabbath? Or was there still a lot of time before the Sabbath? It is so difficult to know, given that we are not even sure of what day it is, and less so of the time that all this happens. But guess what? There is still more to come.

The controversy surrounding the Resurrection

We have seen that there is a current of opinion that maintains that Jesus may have been alive when He was taken down from the cross, which is an exceedingly odd notion in light of the brutal torture that He suffered. Naturally, if He were alive He could hardly have risen from the dead, unless we consider another type of resurrection similar to the *Heb Seb* festivals celebrated by the Pharaohs. But we will come back to that version later on.

Others believe that He died and then rose from the dead. This is the orthodox version. Then there is another, bolder interpretation, which attempts, in one fell swoop, to clear up the contradiction that we have mentioned regarding Jesus' two aspects: the peacemaker and the Jesus who tells his followers to buy a sword. This interpretation holds that in fact there were two very similar persons, so much so that they were twins. Next we will briefly sum up the two heterodox currents of opinion, since we all know the orthodox version of His Death and Resurrection.

Halfway through the 1960s the late Andreas Faber-Kaiser published a book entitled *Jesus Died in Kashmir*. A year later, this book acted as a stimulus for others to embark on their own journalistic adventure, taking on a literary form in books like *The Guardians of the Secret* (Edaf, 2002). Faber-Kaiser's main theory was that Jesus had not died on the cross and that, after having been educated in India during the unknown years of His life, He went to die in the Indian region of Kashmir.

On one occasion, relates Faber-Kaiser, Professor Hassain of Srinagar spoke to him about Jesus and told him that some time ago, during a harsh January month, a snow storm saw him trapped in the region of Ladakh, in the capital Leh, to be more precise. As he had no choice but to stay, he decided to spend his time going through the old local archives. It was thus by chance that he came across the forty volumes of detailed diaries written by the German missionaries Marx and Francke. Both men had attempted to fulfil their mission in the remotest parts of those regions and wrote these diaries in 1894. In the latter a person called San Issa repeatedly appeared, along with the name Nicolai Notovich.

Professor Hassain did not know any German, and so he had to wait until these documents were translated. He finally found out that Notovich, a Russian traveller who travelled the rough land of those parts in the 1880s, had unearthed some manuscripts in the Hemis monastery, 38 kilometers south of Leh. What did those texts speak about? No less than Jesus' alleged journey to India during the years for which the Gospels give us no explanation of His whereabouts.

Of course, such important news aroused Notovich's curiosity, who talked to different Lamas until he discovered that a series of scriptures written in Pali existed and contained a great deal of information about Issa, who appeared to be none other than Jesus of Nazareth. He finally read these documents. He also found out that Issa's tomb was in Srinagar, the capital of Kashmir, and that it is still worshipped today.

However, this story is told more skilfully and carefully by Faber-Kaiser. We suggest that the reader consider to what extent there could be reasons, however miniscule, to think that Jesus could have been taken down from the cross alive.

We have already mentioned some opinions regarding how quickly the Rabbi of Galilee's last moments passed, and how the vessels containing vinegar and honey could have been used as a drug to provoke a state similar to death. Meanwhile, Faber-Kaiser includes in his book quotes from around thirty references from the Indian tradition that *"mention Marham-I-Isa, specifying that this ointment was prepared for Jesus to heal His wounds."* Moreover, the beliefs surrounding the healing of these wounds are weighed up in a quote taken from *The Myth of the Eternal Return* by Mircea Eliade: *"Thus two formulas of incantation, used in England in the sixteenth century at the gathering of simples, state the origin of their therapeutic virtue: they grew for the first time (i.e., ab origine) on the sacred hill of Calvary, at the 'center' of the Earth: 'Haile be thou, holie hearbe, growing on the ground;/all in the mount Caluarie first wert thou found./Thou art good for manie a sore, and healest manie a wound;/in the name of sweet Jesus, I take thee from the ground [1584]. Hallowed be thou, Vervein [verbena], as thou growest on the ground,/for in the Mount of Calvary, there thou wast first found./Thou healedst our Saviour Jesus Christ, and staunchest his bleeding wound...' The effectiveness of these herbs is attributed to the fact that their prototypes were discovered at a decisive cosmic moment (in illo tempore) on Mount Calvary. They received their consecration for having healed the Redeemer's wounds."*

Therefore, Faber-Kaiser attempts to find arguments to support his theory based on the popular tradition that Mircea Eliade includes in his writings. There is even a rumor surrounding some herbs that cured Jesus. Is it true that He recovered and went to die in India? Is His the tomb of Issa? We just do not know.

As we mentioned a few paragraphs earlier, the second theory suggests that Jesus had a twin. More precisely a *Didymus*.

Near the capital of Pakistan, Islamabad, is the site where heterodox historians place Jesus' final resting place.

In the so-called "Gospel of Bartholomew," one of the damned texts that the Church burned—rolling up the sleeves of their cassocks to make the task easier—there are some disturbing words: *"Here is to you, twin of mine, second Christ!"* What on earth does that mean? Of course, if we do not believe this apocryphal text there is not much left to say; peace of mind, you might think. Nevertheless, the Gospels that the Church accepted after the "trance of inspiration" that occurred during the times of Constantine reveal that there are also reasons for suspicion.

John the Evangelist speaks of Thomas, who is called Didymus: *"Then said Thomas, which is called Didymus, unto his fellow disciples..."* (John 11:16); and later: *"Thomas, one of the twelve, called Didymus..."* (John 20:24). Who is Thomas? Apparently he is one of the twelve, and according to tradition he was the one who doubted and had to place his finger into Christ's wounds to believe. Why was it so hard for him to believe that He had risen?

What is most surprising about the matter is that there are some authors who alert us to the idea of *Didymus*, which they translate from the Greek as "twin." So Thomas, the man who doubts, is the blood brother of another person. Of whom?

Following the Resurrection, truly astonishing events take place. As if a man rising from the dead were not enough to amaze us! One of these anomalies is that Mary Magdalene does not recognize Jesus when she sees Him and mistakes Him for the gardener. Why? Has Jesus been mutated in such a way that others do not recognize Him? The fact is that in later appearances He is recognized. Ambelain considers the possibility that Mary Magdalene did not recognize Jesus because He was disguised as a gardener, as if He was afraid of being discovered. How could she be afraid of a spirit, and a divine one at that? Or did she not recognize Him because she saw a man who looked just like Him but dressed differently? Did Mary Magdalene see Jesus' *twin*?

The pilgrims who travel together to Emmaus do not recognize Him at first either. How is that possible? Mark (16:12) recounts a similar event: *"After that He appeared in another form unto two of them, as they walked, and went into the country."* In another form? In what form did He appear before them that they did not recognize Him either? Also, why did the other disciples not believe any of those who said that they had seen Him alive?

Finally, something happens days later that is even harder to believe, when Jesus eats and leaves with His disciples, quite a feat for a resurrected body which is also able to disappear shortly afterwards.

The authors who choose to believe that Jesus did not rise from the dead and claim that He was Thomas' twin conclude the following from all of these strange circumstances: 1) the disciples did not recognize the supposed resurrected Jesus because, quite simply, He was not Jesus; 2) this man eats and drinks because he is a mortal; and 3) they believe that this person is Jesus' blood brother, or *Didymus*, called Thomas.

Ambelain takes a quotation from the so-called "Acts of Thomas," which are apocryphal texts through and through and which may be of interest to us now and later on: *"Thou twin of Christ, apostle of the Most High and initiate in the hidden word of Christ who receivest his secret oracles..."*

In light of these shared reflections, what are we to believe? It is certainly difficult to state one's opinion. In order to avoid making the wrong judgement we would need to wait for one of those "inspirations" that causes the white smoke to rise from the Vatican. However, apart from final conclusions, we have always wondered why, once resurrected, Jesus did not appear before Pontius Pilate and the members of the Sanhedrin and leave them amazed, thereby teaching His followers an unshakeable moral lesson. Why did He wait so long for the Glory of God to fall on the head of all those wretched sceptics?

Juan José Benítez offers quite a different explanation in his saga *Trojan Horse*. Jesus suffered and died on the cross, but the body that rose from the dead was stunned and seemed to require a process of adaptation to the environment, so to speak. This would explain why He was not recognized during the first, magical moments. Maybe that was it.

And if that were not it, then the clever Paul of Tarsus would face a dilemma! *"And if Christ be not risen, then [is] our preaching vain, and your faith [is] also vain. Yea, and we are found false witnesses of God; because we have testified of God that he raised up Christ: whom he raised not up, if so be that the dead rise not. For if the dead rise not, then is not Christ raised: And if Christ be not raised, your faith [is] vain; ye are yet in your sins"* (I Corinthians 15:14-16).

ACT II

Sang Real

"*Verily I say unto you, Wheresoever this gospel shall be preached in the whole world, [there] shall also this, that this woman hath done, be told for a memorial of her.*"

(MATTHEW 23:13)

Mary Magdalene

THERE ARE TEXTS FROM EARLY Christianity, which we will discuss further on, that claim that Mary Magdalene was *"the woman who knew Everything,"* as well as the person who Jesus *"loved more than His disciples."* Can we believe these assertions? If they are true, why did the Church launch a campaign to slander this woman? Was she a sinner? Or a prostitute? Or was she just an extraordinarily important woman and therefore an inconvenience for the male leadership of the new Church?

The ecclesiastical leadership decided that women could not be disrespectful toward them, which meant that they would have no say in the new religion. They only attributed some importance to Mary, Jesus' mother, but they put her on such a high pedestal that other women could not reach her. For instance, we are told that she was impregnated by the Holy Spirit when everyone knows that it is impossible for a virgin to give birth. And so women, as was true since Eve walked around unclothed in the Garden of Eden, were deemed impure. Men, of course, were not. Therefore, the male heads of the Christian Church guaranteed themselves a permanent monopoly on the leadership.

We wonder what reasons, which verge on the obsessive, the Church might have had to put Mary Magdalene, and women in general, in such a humiliating position. We will try to find the answer by considering the theories of various researchers, as well as our own ideas on the matter. However, before we go any further, we should perhaps ask ourselves who was the real Mary Magdalene?

The first surprising fact is that, apart from Jesus' mother, Mary Magdalene is the only other woman to be mentioned by her name—albeit on few occasions—in the canonical Gospels without this being due to her being the wife or sister of a man. In other words, she appears as herself, lending her an air of independence which is certainly challenging for men. Secondly, we could add that she was an exceptional eyewitness to the greatest and most enigmatic moments of Jesus' vague life: His Unction, His Crucifixion, and His Resurrection. We could even state that she was the first "apostle," since it is to her that Jesus entrusted the publication of His Resurrection, at least in part because the men were in hiding and had lost the faith that they had previously shown. Except that Magdalene, and others who were not apostles, knew things that Jesus' so-called disciples did not, quite simply because they were not included in His esoteric circle.

Jesus' time was one in which women were second-class citizens. Men held the top political and religious posts, and so it is not surprising that animosity was caused among the apostles when Jesus included women among His followers and when one of them, *"the one he kissed often upon the lips"* according to the Gnostic texts, took on a leading role.

Aside from the well-known accusation of prostitution that the Church used to stigmatize Mary Magdalene, we do not know much more about her. Of course, this accusation lacks any grounding. Luke (7:36f) mentions the existence of a *"woman of the city, who was a sinner,"* who anoints and washes the Master's feet, which causes the men who witness the scene to protest violently. However, instead of humoring them, Jesus astonishes them by assuring the woman that her sins are forgiven. Was that sinful woman Mary Magdalene? The Evangelist does not say as much, so where did the Church get such an idea?

Mary Magdalene appears in the manuscript of this Evangelist in the following chapter (Luke 8:2). Luke realizes that Jesus was accompanied by *"certain women, which had been healed of evil spirits and infirmities."* He writes that Jesus cured Magdalene after He cast out *"seven devils"* from her. Was this an initiation rite? Authors such as Baigent, Leigh, and Lincoln are inclined to think that it was a typical ritual in the worship of Ishtar or Astarte which *"involved, for example, a seven-stage initiation."* Others prefer to believe that "sinner" meant that she failed to obey the Jewish religion, and that perhaps she followed a different creed. But which one?

In addition, it is surprising that those women mentioned by Luke—who seem to come from the lower social strata—were those who backed Jesus' group, *"which ministered unto him of their substance."* Regarding Magdalene's strong financial standing, rather different from that of a poor prostitute, Lynn Picknett and Clive Prince believe that Magdalene perhaps did not come from a town called Magdala or Mejdel, but that this may be a title that proves the noble lineage of this mysterious lady.

Another widely discussed issue is whether Mary Magdalene could be the woman who performed Jesus' Unction prior to His arrest and Crucifixion, whether she is the aforementioned "sinner," and even whether both are Mary, sister of Lazarus and Martha, residents of the fascinating town of Bethany where all the action seemed to take place. We are going to stay on this point, since it is highly relevant to what may have happened later on.

What do the Evangelists have to say about it? Let us now look at the four different versions of the story to see what sense we can make of the matter. We will let Luke take on the role of narrator. Luke (7:36f) writes about a "repentant sinner" in a Pharisee's house, does not mention the woman's name, and the latter washes Jesus' feet with ointment and wipes them with her hair.

For his part, Matthew (26:6) sets the story in Bethany, although in the house of another of Jesus' mysterious acquaintances in that town, called Simon "the Leper." He speaks of an alabaster box containing *"very precious ointment"*—somewhat out of the reach of a prostitute but typical of a rich woman—but does not name the woman in question. Neither does Mark (14:3). However, John provides many more details. As usual, the town of Bethany makes an appearance, as do the other "disciples" who appear to know a lot more than the apostles were willing to admit. But what story does John tell?

John of Zebedee—if it is he who wrote this mysterious Gospel—states that (11:1-2) it was Mary who anointed Jesus' feet and adds that (12:1-8) *"six days before the Passover"* at her brother Lazarus' house she anointed Jesus with *"a pound of ointment of spikenard, very costly."* The apostles hypocritically reproach her for being wasteful, but Jesus rebukes them with a categorical statement: *"Let her alone: against the day of my burying hath she kept this. For the poor always ye have with you; but me ye have not always."* The day of His burying? What did Mary know that the apostles did not? Maybe, as the Gnostic texts claim, she really did *"know Everything."* Let us go on.

Illustration of Mary Magdalene in contemplative ecstasy, apparently pregnant, in the church of Rennes-le-Château.

The episode seems to prove that Mary of Bethany was the woman who anointed Jesus' feet on both occasions. Therefore it does not appear likely that she was a sinner, since Jesus held her family in high esteem and she seems to have had a high social standing. So, is Mary of Bethany Mary Magdalene? Many authors think not, many others think so. Researchers such as William E. Phipps point out that it is highly surprising that, Mary of Bethany being one of Jesus' faithful followers, none of the Evangelists mention her at the dramatic moment of the Crucifixion.

We will now analyze these horrifying scenes, again using four different versions. You will immediately discover that they all feature lots of women. Where did they all come from since until now in the Gospels Jesus only seemed to be surrounded by men?

Matthew (27:55) tells us that, *"And many women were there beholding afar off, which followed Jesus from Galilee, ministering unto him: Among which was Mary Magdalene, and Mary the mother of James and Joses, and the mother of Zebedee's children."* In other words, there were *"many women"* among Jesus' followers. Why do the Evangelists hide them up until the time of the Crucifixion?

Mark (15:40) also mentions Mary Magdalene and Mary, mother of James the Less and Joses, and Salome. He also writes that they followed Him and served Him, and adds: *"and many other women which came up with him unto Jerusalem."* Where had they been until now in the Gospels?

Luke is more succinct (23:49), as he gives no names but speaks of a group of women who had followed Him. Nonetheless, later he does mention Magdalene in the scene of the empty tomb. Then there is John, and as usual we must read his Gospel carefully since his words are always full of hidden meanings. He writes (John 19:25f): *"Now there stood by the cross of Jesus his mother, and his mother's sister, Mary the [wife] of Cleophas, and Mary Magdalene. When Jesus therefore saw his mother, and the disciple standing by, whom he loved, he saith unto his mother, Woman, behold thy son! Then saith he to the disciple, Behold thy mother! And from that hour that disciple took her unto his own [home]."*

In light of the above, we can say that there is unanimous agreement that Mary Magdalene was there by the cross. Returning to William E. Phipps' arguments, the reason Mary of Bethany is not mentioned on Golgotha is that the person who appears there is Mary Magdalene, who is in fact the same woman, in his opinion.

We would like to stress again Jesus' statement in which He claims that Mary had kept the costly ointment with His burying in mind, and it is precisely Magdalene who is the first person to go to his tomb afterwards. Does this bring new proof to light to identify both women?

Whatever the case, the reader can search the Gospels to find a single reason to believe that Magdalene was a prostitute. Of course, there is none whatsoever. This means that the Church's efforts to spread an idea that still survives today must have been for a different reason. And this reason must have been extremely important, maybe even an argument that could have destabilized the religious doctrine invented later on.

A royal wife

WE CAN IMAGINE TWO REASONS why the Church would tremble at the mere mention of Mary Magdalene. The first is that her role alongside Jesus was more important in all aspects, even on a physical level. The second is that she was the proof that all the ecclesiastical institution said afterwards with regard to Jesus was false, because the Rabbi gave different teachings. We will firstly explore the former theory and later we will look at the second theory regarding a hidden doctrine.

"Do the Gospels provide any information directly or indirectly that gives reason to believe that Jesus was married?" ask the authors of *Holy Blood, Holy Grail*. Their answer is: *"Of course, there is no explicit claim that He was. On the other hand, neither is there to say that He was not."* However, it would seem that many of His apostles, if not all of them, were married. Neither is there explicit mention that Jesus was in favor of celibacy, add these authors. Quite the opposite, since the Gospel according to Matthew says: *"Have ye not read, that he which made [them] at the beginning made them male and female, And said, For this cause shall a man leave father and mother, and shall cleave to his wife: and they twain shall be one flesh?"* (Matthew, 19:4-5). As a result, Baigent, Leigh, and Lincoln conclude that *"these statements are hardly compatible with the recommendation of celibacy. And if Jesus did not preach celibacy, then there is no reason to believe that he practised it."*

We must also add that in those times marriage was not only common for Jewish males, but almost obligatory. Not being married and having no children was not exactly the best way for a man to be taken seriously in his community. This was even less so for a Rabbi, that is, a master or true rabbinical scholar, as Jesus might have been.

Picknett and Prince quote D. H. Lawrence, who wrote about the possible sexual relationship between Jesus and Mary Magdalene in his book *The Man Who Died*. This thorny issue was also explored by Martin Scorsese in his film *The Last Temptation of Christ*, which led to a barrage of criticism against the acclaimed director. And this temptation was only present in Jesus' mind.

Several meters underneath the holy city of Jerusalem hides the truth of what happened in those parts millennia ago.

However, nowhere in the authorized version of the Gospels can we find an explicit mention of this possibility. Of course, this is not the case if we look at the texts that the Church rejected, such as the so-called "Gospel according to Philip." In this, statements such as the following appear regarding Magdalene: *"But Jesus loved her more than all the other disciples, and often kissed her on the mouth..."*

In this statement, authors generally only focus on the obvious sexual nature of the relationship between Jesus and Magdalene, but we are interested in it for an entirely different reason. Note that it says that He *"loved her more than all the other disciples,"* which means that she was included among the disciples. She was not, therefore, a "sinner" or a "prostitute" who appears by chance in the Gospels as a possessed woman willing to anoint Jesus' feet with lotion or kiss His feet like a frenzied fan. Oh, no. We are speaking about a disciple. Just in case this is not clear, the same source later states: *"There were three who always walked with the Lord: Mary, his mother, and his sister, and Magdalene, the one who was called his companion."* There is not much left of the "greatest story ever told," since not only are we informed that Magdalene is a disciple—*"who always walked with the Lord"*—but that she was also his "companion," and that Jesus has at least one "sister," which suggests that Mary's ongoing virginial condition is truly miraculous.

The Hidden "Lives" of Jesus contains theories that Jesus and Mary Magdalene—who we have pointed out may be Mary of Bethany, sister of Martha and Lazarus—got married and that this was the wedding that according to the Gospels took place in Cana, Galilee. Could it be possible?

On one occasion, the Franciscans, guardians of the Holy Land, held a mass in this town of Cana at which they invited the couples present to renew their vows in a symbolic ceremony. Afterwards, at the church exit, the persons present at the mock event waited for them with handfuls of rice, as if the couple had really been married there. Meanwhile, close by, a stone jar reminded them of what had happened two thousand years ago, if we are to believe the Evangelists, when water in six stone jars was turned into good wine.

Why was Jesus' mother concerned that there was no wine left if she was only a guest? Why did she ask Jesus to do something about it when He had not yet performed a miracle that showed that He had come in the name of the Father? Was there not a better time for that than in the midst of such merriment? Finally, why did the servants do what Mary told them: *"Do whatever he tells you"*? This would only be understandable if they were usually under her command.

Whom did Jesus marry? Opinions center on two possible candidates in this story: Mary of Bethany or Mary Magdalene. But we said that they were the same woman. Both loved Jesus according to the aforementioned texts. Furthermore, both seem to be rich. Mary of Bethany definitely was, and Mary Magdalene must have been as well, since she is said to have financially supported Jesus' and His followers' adventures.

If Magdalene and Mary of Bethany were the same person, according to *Holy Blood, Holy Grail* this would explain why, when Jesus arrives in Bethany and Lazarus is already dead, it is Martha who goes to meet Him and tells Him that, had He been there, he would not have died. It seems that Mary does not leave the house: *"Then Martha, as soon as she heard that Jesus was coming, went and met him: but Mary sat still in the house"* (John 11:20). The same authors explain this by claiming that Mary was sitting *shiveh*; in other words, she was mourning. They go on to state that *"according to the principles of Jewish Law at that time, it was forbidden for a woman 'sitting shiveh' to leave the house under the express orders of her husband."* Strangely enough, in the Gospel according to John, Mary leaves the house after her sister has spoken to Jesus. Martha returns to the house and tells her that the Master has arrived. Immediately Mary rushes out and falls at His feet weeping.

The most daring version of these events is to be found in *Bloodline of the Holy Grail*, in which the author does not hesitate to make statements that make us feel ignorant and turn us into second-rate heterodoxes. He claims that two wedding ceremonies, so to speak, took place in those times. The second ritual confirmed what the bride and bridegroom had declared in the first. According to this author: *"...Jesus' first wedding took place in September 30 AD, His thirty-sixth September, the exact time when, according to Luke, 7:37-38, Mary Magdalene anointed His feet for the first time."*

If you find this statement troubling, then read the following: *"Anyway, no conception took place (...) But in December of the following year, Mary Magdalene became pregnant and, as was the rule, once again anointed Jesus' feet and head in Bethany (...) the second wedding officially taking place in March 33 AD."*

From here on we start to slip uncontrollably down an emotional slide. During the imminent vertiginous descent the reader should decide whether they prefer a free fall or, in the interest of the health of their bones of faith, they wish to hang on tightly to the old principles of catechism. They can do as they prefer...or whichever hurts the least. As for us, we are going to try to delve deeper into the keys to *The Da Vinci Code*.

Jesus' tomb in Jerusalem. According to tradition, this was in Joseph of Arimathea's garden. Who knows...?

The most worrying thing about this whole imbroglio is not just that Jesus was not as the Church claims He was. Even the fact that He was married would not be a time bomb ready to explode. The worst thing about the whole affair is what Teabing—one of the characters in *The Da Vinci Code*—explains to Sophie: *"...Not only was Jesus Christ married, but He was a father. My dear, Mary Magdalene was the Holy Vessel. She was the chalice that bore the royal bloodline of Jesus Christ. She was the womb that bore the lineage, and the vine from which the sacred fruit sprang forth!"*

Before the reader has time to recover from the shocking news that Jesus Christ and Mary Magdalene had a child, we must add that some authors claim that there was not only one child, but three children. One such example is Gardner. He displays unlimited knowledge—or boldness—when he says that *"Mary Magdalene was three months pregnant at the time of the Crucifixion."* He continues, unperturbed: *"...six months after the Crucifixion, on 15 September 33 AD, it was Jesus' thirty-ninth official birthday and in that month a daughter was born to Mary Magdalene. She was named Tamar [Palm tree—assimilated in Greek to the name Damaris], a traditional Davidic family name."* The author then states that Jesus—who of course was not considered to be dead on the cross—was finally admitted to the priesthood, a ritual in which He "ascended into heaven" in his opinion, in accordance with old principles that he tries to explain as best as he can. Three years later He returns to Mary Magdalene and she has her second child, who they call Jesus. But don't go away just yet, there is still more to come...

All of the above happened in approximately the spring of 44 AD. The same author affirms that *"Jesus set out to carry out a mission in Galatia, in the central region of Asia Minor, along with John Mark..."* Meanwhile, the Nazarene sect of which the apostle James was leader at that time began to pose a threat to Rome, although the author does not explain why. The fact is that Herod Antipas reacted on behalf of the Romans and claimed James of Zebedee as their prize. The latter was taken by the disciples who sailed with his body to Iria Flavia, and thus triggered the famous pilgrimages to Galicia. But in the meantime, what happened to Mary Magdalene according to this version of the story?

Like so many others, Mary Magdalene was in danger, but with the further difficulty that she was—for the third time—pregnant. This child was to be *"the child of the Holy Grail"* according to Gardner. Magdalene appealed to Herod Agrippa II, the King's son, and was allowed to secretly leave Palestine for Gaul, where we are told that Herod Antipas and Archelaus were banished. Gardner also states that *"Mary gave birth to her second child"*—he refers to her second son since she already had a daughter and a son—*"in Provence in that same year."*

In Gardner's opinion, when the Acts of the Apostles state that *"So mightily grew the word of God and prevailed"* (Acts 19:20), we should understand that it was Jesus' bloodline that grew. A forced interpretation? We think so.

Whatever the case, it is clear that there is a current of opinion on which Dan Brown based his ideas when he wrote *The Da Vinci Code*. Regardless of whether this line of study alludes to one child or more, or whether it claims that Jesus died on the cross or not, the fact remains that it is a truly heterodox line according to which the Holy Grail is no other than royal blood: *sang real*.

The question now is whether this is due to Jesus' supposed lineage from King David or, as an imaginative Dan Brown suggests, this bloodline was fused with that of Mary Magdalene, who according to this novelist descended from the House of Benjamin. In other words, Magdalene is also a descendant of Kings. This is explained by the mysterious and erudite Teabing in the book: *"By marrying into the powerful house of Benjamin, Jesus fused two royal bloodlines, creating a potent political union with the potential of making a legitimate claim to the throne and restoring the line of kings as it was under Solomon."*

Why is this point important? *Holy Blood, Holy Grail* explains the situation in much the same way. Saul, the first King of Israel, was of the

House of Benjamin. His heir, David, was from the tribe of Judah; In Benjamite eyes this might have rendered him a usurper, and so the merging of the twelve tribes would be difficult under the command of a son of Judah such as Jesus was, since He descended from David. However, if a prince of Judah married a princess of the tribe of Benjamin, in this case Mary Magdalene, the situation would change significantly since their heirs would indeed receive consent from all the clans.

We will leave this string of reasoning for the time being, but we will later use it to guide us through the labyrinth that awaits us. Right now we will give in to two temptations. One concerns the consequences of Mary Magdalene being Mary of Bethany. The other refers to what Mary Magdalene might have known that the other disciples did not, but to find this out we will have to wait until the third act of this incredible story.

The Beloved Disciple

LET US IMAGINE THAT MARY MAGDALENE AND MARY OF BETHANY are one disturbing being. What family repercussions

The Wailing Wall. Centuries ago the Knights Templar searched for part of the secret here...

46

would this have? Well, Lazarus and Martha are brother and sister to Magdalene, and consequently, following the wedding at Cana, they are Jesus' brother and sister-in-law.

Lazarus is a useful character for finding out more about the secret doctrine that Jesus only taught to a few. Even the four Evangelists, especially John, mention Jesus' friendship with this family. Furthermore, it is from their house in Bethany that He leaves for His glory or death. It is here that the plan is hatched for Him to take a donkey and ride into Jerusalem to fulfil the king's prophecy. And this house is also the setting for the Unction, which can be interpreted in many different ways. To sum up, Bethany saw quite a bit of action take place.

Secondly, Lazarus is one of the few mortals who rose from the dead without being a god or anything similar. We are simply told that he left the tomb, bandages and all. Resurrection not being a frequent event among humans, our attention is drawn to him.

Why did Jesus take two days to reach Bethany when He was notified that Lazarus was sick? Did He do it to raise him from the dead afterwards? Or was it that, as we mentioned earlier, this death was not physical but ritual and Lazarus had to remain isolated for a certain amount of time? We will never know, but we will not deny that there are even more shocking interpretations of this event. However, we will not go into them here. The fact remains that this resurrection makes Lazarus someone special.

In fact, Lazarus was so special that John the Evangelist refers to him as *"the disciple whom Jesus loved."* Jesus must have held him in high esteem and entrusted him with missions rather than giving them to the other disciples, because only this would explain why the Sanhedrin was driven to murder him according to John (12:10-11): *"But the chief priests consulted that they might put Lazarus also to death; Because that by reason of him many of the Jews went away, and believed on Jesus."* Was it just because Lazarus was proof of Jesus' powers? Or maybe because he was one of the main members of Jesus' group of followers? We are inclined to think the latter.

Yet the Sanhedrin, Pontius Pilate, and the others do not seem to be bothered about the rest of the Apostles. No one would have wasted a good pair of sandals on seizing impetuous and proud Peter or fine swordsman Simon the Zealot. So why would they focus on Lazarus?

Earlier we made it clear that Jesus' true circle of initiates were those who remained faithful—perhaps because they played a specific role in the plot, according to some people—during the time of the Crucifixion. If Mary Magdalene was near the cross, why not think that her brother Lazarus was next to her?

And what if we read John's statement about Lazarus—*"the disciple whom Jesus loved"*—and we compare it with what he writes about the time of the Crucifixion—*"...When Jesus therefore saw his mother, and the disciple standing by, whom he loved..."*—are they similar? We think so. Can we conclude that Lazarus was in fact "the beloved disciple"? Did Lazarus use the pseudonym John to write the darkest and most secretive

Illustrations of the Temple's holy objects appear continually.

Gospel of the four accepted by the Church, in which it so happens that all of these characters supposedly play a secondary role? Why does John never mention himself with that name? What hidden teaching does he slip into his book?

Leaving the foregoing aside, we are going to continue on the trail of the "child of the Holy Grail" and her mother during their trip to France. We will discover that Lazarus was also there, as was Joseph of Arimathea; in other words, all the truly mysterious characters in this extremely involved plot.

However, there is an even more astonishing version of the events that may reveal the identity of the evasive "beloved disciple." Later we will discuss Leonardo Da Vinci and his work "The Last Supper."

The Grail quest

IN SOUTH-EAST FRANCE there are many legends—some claim there are even archaeological remains—according to which some time after the Crucifixion Mary Magdalene and other relatives, probably including Lazarus—her brother if we believe that Magdalene and Mary of Bethany were the same person—arrived in the Provence region. In the book *The Templar Revelation* we are told that the number of persons accompanying Mary Magdalene varies according to different traditions. Some mention Mary Salome and Mary Jacobe; others even claim that she was accompanied by Maximinus. The latter was supposedly one of Jesus' seventy-two disciples and became the first Bishop of Provence and later a saint, thus carving out a brilliant career for himself. However, there are two highly interesting characters to be added to the list. Firstly, a black servant called Sara, who we will now study, and secondly the most mysterious man of them all: Joseph of Arimathea.

In that region of the Roman Empire, in what is now France, there was an important Jewish community. It is said that even the Herod family had an interest there.

According to heretic tradition, Mary Magdalene was carrying Jesus' child. Aside from claims by authors such as Gardner that she might have had other children previously, most researchers who believe in these ideas speak about the "child of the Holy Grail" when they refer to this baby, regardless of whether it was a boy or a girl. Nonetheless, the Church, which had no choice but to admit that Magdalene was present in this region, attempted to mould the image of her to make it more presentable to parishioners. They did this as follows.

If we believe the legend that maintains that the newcomers arrived at what is now Saintes-Maries-de-la-Mer in the Camargue region, the Church turned her into a hermit of unshakeable faith and invented the improbable story that she lived in a cave, in Sainte-Baume. Why would they do that? Because the Church had it in for Mary Magdalene and continued to persecute her for being a prostitute and a sinner. Therefore, in view of the devotion that the town showed towards her— apparently in that region she preached to the people with outstanding success—they decided to have her become a hermit which would allow her sins to be forgiven. However, there may be other hidden interests behind this idea.

Indeed, according to Picknett and Price the idea that Magdalene lived as an anchorite in the famous cave in this region is not even accepted by *"the present verger of the Catholic Church."* If this is the case, why the interest in her living and expiating her sins in this cave? The same authors provide an answer, which may indeed be the right one: *"the Church folded Sainte-Baume into the Magdalena Legend looking for a parallel with the life of another prostitute and saint, St. Mary of Egypt, and in which Magdalene was supposedly present. That cave was the shrine of a pagan god. The story was clever in two ways: it turned an independent person such as Magdalene into a conventional saint and a former pagan shrine into a site that attracted Christian pilgrims."* We say that these authors may be right because this conduct is typical of the Church, whose calendar of saints' days is full of wizards, sorcerers, and sorceresses that the people held in high regard and worshipped, and for whom the clergy made up a custom-designed saintly life so that it seemed that they were theirs. But going back to Mary Magdalene...

Whether she lived in this cave or not, the fact is that the whole region, and other neighboring regions that we will mention below, knew about her existence and, worse still for the Church, of her vast apostolic work. Indeed, we have already stated that she must have been the leading spokesperson for Jesus' doctrine. Furthermore, it is strange that in that area, especially in Arles, there was a long-standing worship of the Egyptian Goddess Isis, an issue we will pick up again further on.

Saintes-Maries-de-la-Mer is home to the church of Notre-Dame de la Mer. Inside this church three Marys are venerated: Mary Magdalene, Mary Jacobe and Mary Salome. There is also a chapel dedicated to the strange Egyptian servant called Sara that we mentioned earlier in passing and who, as it happens, was black. Why did those people worship a servant? Or was she not a servant? Did they worship her for being black? And why would they do that? Was she linked to the old tradition of worshipping the Goddess Isis who is often represented with a dark complexion? Are we heading towards black virgins? Of course! But we will take that road later on. For the time being we will mention that every year, on May 25, the Gypsies gather in the Camargue to appoint the "Gypsy Queen of the Year" in front of the mysterious statue of Sara.

Moreover, there are also traces of Mary Magdalene's presence in Marseilles. Picknett and Price claim that the place where she usually preached was precisely *"on the steps of an ancient Temple of the Goddess Diana"*; i.e. another evident allusion to the ancient worship of the Goddess. They go on to say that there is nothing left of this sanctuary, but it appears to have once been on the present site of the Place de Lanche.

The legend grows longer, and says that Mary Magdalene died in Saint-Maximin-la-Sainte-Baume and that—pay heed to the information and remember it for when we speak about the Templars later!—

every year there is a procession during which her skull is exhibited, which is kept in the vestry during the rest of the year.

While we are on the subject of the relics of Mary Magdalene, it is worthwhile looking at their connection with the House of Anjou since, as you will see, this noble lineage is also linked to the possible guardians of the Grail. We will try to briefly describe the background to make it easier to understand what we want to explain.

It would appear that halfway through the 13th century one of King Saint Louis' hobbies was collecting relics, perhaps because there was no

The Black Virgin of Rocamadour, more than just a sculpture.

room for more intellectual entertainment in his head. Having heard the rumor that Mary Magdalene was buried in Vézelay, he set off in that direction and, using the advantage of his royal position, ordered that her bones be put on display.

We imagine that the monks broke out in a cold sweat and perhaps let out a weak laugh. What could they do? In our opinion, they knew that the relics were not there and had spread the rumor in order to make the sanctuary famous. Consequently, the king was tricked and given a metal chest containing what could have been anyone's bones. However, among the persons present at that complete farce was Saint Louis' nephew, Charles of Anjou, who became fascinated and later obsessed with the matter. Why?

The aforementioned sources relate that years later Charles of Anjou ordered the crypt in Saint-Maximin to be excavated because he had received a tip-off—or had found out via credible sources linked to the Guardians of the Grail—that the bones of the once-beautiful Jewish lady were there. It is said that he was personally involved in the excavation, even helping the digging with his own hands. In the end, on December 9, 1279, when he was Second Count of Anjou, a 5th century alabaster sarcophagus appeared along with a skeleton and some documents that explained everything. Apparently the Jewish lady's bones had been in another sarcophagus until the year 710, but were moved to the latter site to be better protected.

Charles II of Anjou, in an excited state, naively decided that Christians around the world should go there to worship Magdalene. He dug deep in his pockets and came up with lots of money to build a large basilica. The building work started in 1295, but other pilgrimage destinations, especially Compostela, thwarted his plans.

Nonetheless, what motive drove this count to search so eagerly for Magdalene's final resting place and to honor her memory to this extreme?

As it happens, one of his heirs, René of Anjou, who was around in the 15th century, was linked to the esoteric world and was a devout follower of Mary Magdalene. He was also said to be a Grand Master of the Priory of Sion, a society that hid the conspiracy that we are going to try to tell over the next few pages.

The authors of *Holy Blood, Holy Grail* tell us that he was a highly educated person, quite ahead of his time, and was very interested in the occult. His court included Christopher Columbus for a while, as well as an astrologer, cabalist, and Jewish physician called Jean de Saint-Rémy, who was apparently Nostradamus' grandfather. However, the best thing about the case is that the legends say that he was obsessed with the stories surrounding the Holy Grail and that he had a red crystal goblet that he boasted was used during the weddings at Cana, which he had obtained in Marseilles. In addition, it is said that it bore an inscription:

> *"He who drinks well*
> *will see God. He who quaffs at a single drop*
> *will see God and the Magdalen."*

Although what we are about to say we should probably leave for later on, we think we should deal with it now so the reader will see how the links of this chain seem to fit together. Therefore, we ask you to be indulgent and pay attention.

While René of Anjou was at the court of Cosimo de Médici in Italy, around 1439, all kinds of beliefs were promoted and the local library was filled with strange manuscripts. Furthermore, according to Baigent, Leigh, and Lincoln, René of Anjou added to this knowledge *"one of his favorite symbolic themes: the Theme of Arcadia."* The same authors claim that this nobleman often organized shows on his land in which the theme of the mythical Arcadia was a constant feature. Often this mysterious region was represented in which there was a tombstone and fountain linked to an underground river called Alpheius. The course of this river, considered to be holy since far-off times, carries clear esoteric implications which could be compared to secret knowledge over the centuries.

Let us now leave this story about Arcadia and the Anjou family's devotion to the Holy Grail and Mary Magdalene, and go back to the latter, who we have seen might have arrived at Gaul accompanied by others.

Over the course of this book the ancient ideas regarding Arcadia and the Holy Grail will come back from the grave...

We said earlier that according to tradition, Mary Magdalene did not land in Provence alone. She was probably accompanied by her brother Lazarus and other women. But we also mentioned Joseph of Arimathea.

Joseph of Arimathea

LITTLE IS KNOWN ABOUT THIS MAN. We imagine he was rich, since he was the owner of the tomb in which Jesus' body was buried. He was also an influential person, given that he intervened with Pontius Pilate for Jesus' body to be taken down from the cross. Of course it was very rare that this permission was granted since, according to some authors, it was not usually permitted for a crucified body to be buried.

Facade dedicated to Saint Mary Magdalene, like many other religious buildings linked to the Temple.

There are some aspects of this story that are hard to believe. Joseph of Arimathea was obviously one of Jesus' disciples judging by his actions. However, we are told that he was a secret disciple. Secret in what sense? If this means that he was afraid to be identified as such because he was a member of the Sanhedrin, then we do not understand how he had the courage to go and talk to Pontius Pilate in person. It is clear that at that moment he revealed his Christian identity, is it not? So what do they mean by a secret disciple? *"And after this Joseph of Arimathaea, being a disciple of Jesus, but secretly for fear of the Jews..."* (John 19:38).

Our theory is that Joseph of Arimathea, along with Mary Magdalene, Lazarus, and Nicodemus, *inter alia*, were in fact the disciples of the *Secret Doctrine* that Jesus taught. The supposed apostles had no idea of this doctrine, or, if they did, they did not understand it at all. It is not by chance that one verse later (John 19:39) the mysterious Nicodemus arrives at the tomb, with whom Jesus had had a conversation about initiatory death: *"And there came also Nicodemus, which at the first came to Jesus by night, and brought a mixture of myrrh and aloes, about an hundred pound [weight]."*

All the Evangelists mention Joseph of Arimathea at this specific and significant moment, since this was when it was revealed who was loyal to the Rabbi and who was not. And, as usual, the apostles went away with their tails between their legs showing all their cowardice. None of them appear at the Crucifixion, except maybe "the beloved disciple," whose identity is still not clear. None of them dare to ask for Jesus' body, except for someone who was among His disciples *"secretly."* Only John, in the most esoteric Gospel of the four and in which these mysterious disciples who have settled in Bethany play an important role, mentions Nicodemus' presence, who moreover appears laden down with myrrh and aloe. Is this not excessive for a corpse?

Whatever the case, Joseph of Arimathea carried some spectacular knowledge in his knapsack. According to later tradition he was the guardian of the Holy Grail, although we should probably firstly explain what we mean by the Grail, an explanation that will come shortly. In the meantime, authors such as Gardner turn to the *Annales Ecclesiastici*, which date from 1601, to remind us that cardinal Baronius, a Vatican librarian, claimed that Joseph of Arimathea arrived in Marseilles in 35 AD, and that from there he went to Britain to preach the Gospel. Other versions suggest later dates for this journey.

The same author speaks about the cold welcome that Joseph of Arimathea received from the Britons, although King Arviragus, brother of Caractacus the Pendragon, greeted him with cordiality and even granted him land to build a church in what would become Glastonbury.

Saint John the Evangelist, the chosen one displaced by Jesus?

Later, new buildings were erected forming a full-scale convent and religious complex. Of course, where better to set the legend of the Holy Grail in medieval times. What a coincidence, don't you think?

The secret doctrine

"Sophie, the Priory's tradition of perpetuating goddess worship is based on a belief that powerful men in the early Christian Church 'conned' the world by propagating lies that devalued the female and tipped the scales in favor of the masculine…"

This statement appears in *The Da Vinci Code* and takes us directly on to another deep secret of this plot. It also introduces an organization that we have only mentioned briefly, the Priory of Sion, which we will keep behind the curtain for a little while longer. For the time being we will focus on the aforementioned goddess worship, since we are perhaps closer to what happened two thousand years ago in Palestine than we thought.

Although we have already said the following, we will repeat ourselves: few, maybe none, of the teachings with which the Gospels regale us are original. In the mysterious Egyptian religions there is proof of all this and much more. There are too many examples to list, but we will mention an event that we have discovered took place in Cana, about which theologian Llogari Pujol says *"the Egyptian tomb of Paheri—1500 BC—represents the turning of water into wine by the Pharaoh."* There is a bas-relief that shows that six jugs were used for the occasion, as happens in the Gospel. He also writes that the multiplying of loaves and fishes was already performed by the god Sobk, as recounted in the "Pyramid Texts." This crocodile-headed god, as if this were not astonishing enough, walked on Lake Faiun leaving his followers with their mouths open.

In short, there are many similarities between Christianity and the magical world of Egyptian religion. Indeed, we have already alluded to the similarity between Jesus' Resurrection and the *Heb Sed* celebrations of the Pharaohs. Now it is time to go into more depth regarding the relationship between Jesus and Mary Magdalene and between Osiris and Isis.

We do not need to re-stress that Mary Magdalene, as Jesus' wife, is similar to Isis in that this goddess was Osiris' wife. Neither do we need to say that her special role at the time of the Resurrection is similar to Isis recovering the pieces of her dead husband's body—with the exception of his penis. However, we would like to look at one key aspect, that is if we are to believe the daring theories that we have mentioned above, which is that both had a child. Let us be reasonable and say that

Magdalene had one child, at least. In the case of Isis and Osiris this child was called Horus, and was often represented sitting on his mother's lap.

In far-off times in the kingdom of Israel, Astarte was one of the favorites, and it is said that Solomon allowed the people to worship this Goddess who was deeply rooted at the very core of their faith. Further back in time, according to *The Templars and the Lost Word* (Edaf, 2003), people looked on Mother Earth as the goddess who would inspire them with confidence and give them affection, and they represented her in the form of clay figurines that prehistorians call *Venus*. These were basic female shapes in which the breasts and sexual organs were accentuated, which represented fertility, the key to survival.

According to Price and Picknett, *"all the mysterious schools of Osiris, Tammuz, Dionysus, Attis, and others included a rite (...) in which the goddess anointed the god as a preliminary act before the actual or symbolic death, which was used to fertilise the land once more."* They go on to say: *"Traditionally, after three days had passed and following the magical intervention of the priestess/goddess, he rose from the dead and the people could breathe a sigh of relief until the following year."*

In light of these thousand-year-old rituals that Jesus may have learned in Egypt, could it be said that Mary Magdalene was a priestess or initiate in mysterious rites, and that Jesus and she represented a specific thousand-year-old ritual? Is that why Mary Magdalene was the disciple who *"knew Everything,"* as some Gnostic texts claim?

In the myth about Osiris, he rises from the dead following the intervention of Isis. In Jesus' Resurrection, the first person to arrive at the tomb and witness the miracle is Magdalene. If we continue to draw these comparisons, would it not be perfectly logical that the fertility ritual was part of this cult? This same question is asked by the sources that Dan Brown quotes in *The Da Vinci Code* who conclude that perhaps the statues of Our Lady Holding the Baby Jesus represented in Christianity are just a poor imitation of Isis holding Horus. These do not represent Mary holding the Baby Jesus but Magdalene holding the heir. But do all of these statues carry this hidden meaning? Are all the statues of Our Lady Holding the Baby Jesus really Magdalene and her child? Their answer is no. They are possibly those that iconography represented as black virgins, which we will study now.

The ancient goddess, Earth, who was called Isis, Astarte, Diana, Demeter, or Cibeles, was a hard nut to crack for the Church. Therefore, the latter attempted to employ the old tactic of giving her that identity and made Mary, Jesus' mother, a virgin. However, the hidden tradition could not have felt comfortable with that idea, since fertility could hardly be extolled through virginity, and the heretics chose Mary Magdalene, the mother of Jesus' child—or children, according to different versions.

Isis and Magdalene; more than a coincidence?

There are more than four hundred examples of the Black Virgins around the world, in Gardner's opinion. A study carried out by Ean Begg in 1985 shows that 65% of these statues are in France, mainly in the south. It was in this large region that Mary Magdalene was worshipped fervently, not only in Provence but also in Languedoc, where we will now stop to speak about Cathars and Templars, followed by the murky issue of Rennes-le-Château.

Something about these virgins makes the Church feel awkward, which is perhaps why they painted some of them black and could explain what happened in 1952, as described by Ean Begg in his book *The Cult of the Black Virgin* (1985): *"The hostility was unmistakable on December 28, 1952, when papers about the Black Madonnas were going to be presented to the American Association for the Progress of Science. All the priests and nuns in the audience got up and left the room."*

Why this attitude? And why are they black?

It has been said that this is because the statues darken with the inexorable passing of time, they become damaged if they are exposed to the smoke from candles, or because they are carved from materials such as ebony, etc. But there is another theory, presented by the enigmatic Fulcanelli in his book *The Mystery of Cathedrals*. He explains that, since time immemorial, the Mother Earth in the form of Isis was worshipped in the places where many of these large buildings were erected. He adds: *"Prior to the conception, in the astronomical theogony Isis is the attribute of the Virgin that several documents, much earlier than Christianity, call 'Virgo pariturae,' in other words, 'the earth before fertilisation,'"* which soon will be brought to life by the rays of the Sun.*"* Thus, the earth must be fertilized and, as Nacho Ares reminds us, for the Egyptians the color black represented fertility since the mud of the River Nile is this same color. Furthermore, whether we like it or not, there is an intrinsic link between the places of worship of Mary Magdalene and these black sculptures. The aforementioned Begg claims to have discovered no fewer than fifty places of Magdalene worship, which also include a sanctuary where a Black Virgin lies. In *The Templar Revelation* we are told: *"Investigations revealed an astonishing concentration of Black Madonnas in the area of Lyons/Vichy/Clermont/Ferrand, focused on the hills known as the Monts de la Madeleine (the Magdalene's Hills). And all around the eastern Pyrenees and Provence, where there are enduring legends that she came to live out her long life, there are also high concentrations of statues of Black-faced Virgins and their children."*

We would like to add just one more idea to the foregoing. We have stated that there was a group of people—Magdalene, Lazarus, Nicodemus, Joseph of Arimathea—who were perhaps the true receivers of the secret teachings given by Jesus as a religious leader. We have also mentioned that, also being a political leader, a group of armed men may have formed his ring of safety, who did not know anything about philosophy. Therefore, that secret doctrine, ancient Knowledge, or Wisdom would be no other than the *Sophia* to which the Gnostic texts refer. Moreover, according to Tradition, that Wisdom is black.

"Dark am I, yet lovely..." reads "The Song of Solomon" (1:5), a work attributed to the wise sorcerer king whose ultimate ambition was to attain Wisdom. Solomon was an alchemist, cabalist, and controller of the forces of Nature, and this work inspired Bernard of Claraval, the head of the Order of the Temple, to write dozens of sermons. What a coincidence!

Guardians of the Grail

"And said, Hitherto shalt thou come, but no further..."

(JOB 38:11)

The Holy Grail

IN ORDER TO UNDERSTAND THE KEYS TO DAN BROWN'S NOVEL, the version of the Grail legend to consider is the following, as described by Baigent, Leigh, and Lincoln: *"the Holy Grail is at least two things at once."* Firstly, there is the Royal Blood, the child of Jesus and Mary Magdalene, in other words, *Sang Real*. Secondly, the Grail is the receptacle that caught Jesus' blood, understood to be Mary Magdalene's womb. The chalice, therefore, would be her body. As we will see when we discuss Leonardo da Vinci further on, this recipient was shown in the shape of a "V," strangely enough the first letter of the goddess par excellence: Venus.

However, to complete the version that the novelist supports, the Grail could have one further meaning. According to the authors of *The Messianic Legacy,* this would be as follows: *"The Messiah had to be a priest-king whose authority encompassed spiritual and secular domains alike. It is thus likely, indeed probable, that the temple housed official records pertaining to Israel's royal line—the equivalents of the birth certificates, marriage licenses, and other relevant data concerning any modern royal or aristocratic family. If Jesus was indeed 'King of the Jews,' the temple is almost certain to have contained copious information relating to him."*

The main male character in the novel, Robert Langdon, tells Sophie that *"For a thousand years legends of this secret have been passed on. The entire collection of documents, its power, and the secret that it reveals have been known by a single name—Sangreal."*

Therefore, the search for these documents and their subsequent location have become the quest for the Grail. Was it for that purpose that the Knights Templar went to Jerusalem centuries later?

Before we go on we would like to add that we are giving this version of the Grail legend by way of explanation so that the reader may understand the ins and outs of the works that put forward this theory, such as *The Da Vinci Code*. This is not necessarily how we interpret the Grail or the cause of the Templar quest; indeed, we have already suggested further

MARIANO FERNÁNDEZ URRESTI AND LORENZO FERNÁNDEZ BUENO

alternatives in other books. Nevertheless, we will now return to the matter in hand and follow the trail of the *Sang Real*.

The damned dynasty

IF WE CHOOSE TO BELIEVE THE THEORY that we have briefly described above, Mary Magdalene arrived in France carrying a child. No more is known about Jesus for certain, although some people claim he was in Kashmir, as we mentioned earlier, or in Egypt; then again, others think they can trace his steps in France, whether he was alive or dead. Furthermore, Richard Andrews and Paul Schellenberger claim to have located his tomb on Mount Cardou, in the vicinity of the "accursed town" of Rennes-le-Château.

Let us leave Jesus to one side and focus on the genealogical line that, according to all of these researchers, started with His child who would consequently have been a descendant of the House of David if, as the Gospels state, Jesus descended from the mythical King David.

So, if we appeal to the possibility that these disconcerting events actually took place and we could condense the story right down, the result might look something like the following.

Theories surrounding the matter maintain that Jesus' family, just like many other Jewish families, settled in the southeast of France and enjoyed a certain amount of prestige in the region. The passing of time brought with it unpleasant surprises for the Church, and the events took place far from here.

A community of Germanic origin known as the Sicambrians, who were among the vast conglomerate of tribes called the Franks, settled in the regions of present day Germany and France following the migration flows caused by the Gothic impulse and the weakness of the Roman Empire in its death throes. It is said that the Sicambrian people gave rise to the Merovingian dynasty. We are speaking about the late 5th and early 6th centuries. As it happens, this coincides with the era of King

Arthur in Britain, where it was said that Joseph of Arimathea arrived with his mythical bundle containing the Holy Grail.

The source of the Merovingian name, which gradually gained control of France, was their mythical founder Meroveus. Naturally, legend has it that he came from a spectacular background, having been born from two fathers, one of them a sea monster, no less. It was said that his mother, who was pregnant by King Clodion, decided to go for a swim in the sea and was raped by a monster of unknown origin but with apparently human-like characteristics. According to this legend, Meroveus carried holy blood and divine blood, since it was decided that the rapist was a relative of Neptune. The fact that the holy blood comes from the sea is something that seems to be repeated time and again throughout the various versions of this story.

In light of the foregoing, it is not surprising that the first Merovingian kings were cloaked in fantastic legends. They were considered to be priest-kings, shamans capable of working miracles and, according to Leigh, Baigent, and Lincoln, *"they all supposedly bore a distinctive birthmark, which distinguished them from all other men (...) and which attested to their semidivine or sacred blood. This birthmark reputedly took the form of a red cross, either over the heart—a curious anticipation of the Templar blazon—or between the shoulder blades."*

Their many peculiarities included the belief that, like Samson, their strength lay in their hair, which meant that they did not include hairdressers among their friends and they were eventually called the "Long-Haired Kings." As we will see, this was not the only Semitic custom that they upheld. Apart from being similar to the Pharaohs in that they held both political and religious power, they considered themselves to be the incarnation of God. According to them, they were of divine origin. But where did they actually come from?

Many argue that they came from Troy—which would explain place names in the north of France linked to the Trojan War such as Troyes and Paris. Others claims that they came from the Arcadia region in

Greece—an area that we mentioned earlier and to which we will come back further on. There are even theories that they were descendants of the evasive Jewish tribe of Benjamin.

Clovis is the most famous and perhaps the most important of the monarchs. He ruled from 482 to 511 and, after defeating the Gallic-Roman Duke Syagrius in 486, he did away with what little there was left of the imperial heritage. Afterwards, all went well for good old Clovis until his wife Clotilde decided to get involved in his religious life. Although this might not seem to be a significant event, it actually is. Indeed, in those times Catholicism was not the main religious and political player in convulsed Europe, but Aryanism was. This religious version of Christianity, which of course the Church repressed as far as it could under the name of heresy, had been preached by a priest from Alexandria— where we stated that centuries earlier Jesus learned doctrines and knowledge inherited from the mysterious Egyptians— called Arius. What else would he be called?

Consecration of King Clovis by Saint Remigius, according to F. Mateáis.

So what did Arius have to say? Well, he suggested a similar version of Jesus as the Gnostic texts; that is, that He was an extraordinary master but that He was only a man. He claimed that Jesus Christ was a creation of God, therefore he was not eternal and was distinct from Him. In other words, Jesus was not a God. This idea appealed to the kings of the time far more than the product being sold by Paul's followers in which Jesus appeared as a God. As a result, and although Aryanism was condemned by the Roman Church on several occasions, the regions that came to be occupied by the Swabians, Vandals, Alans, Merovingians, and all the other people that have been labelled "the Barbarians," were Arian. The newcomers embraced those beliefs, the same beliefs that Clovis held when he said his prayers before going to bed, until his wife Clotilde began to interfere.

Nevertheless, the real problem went deeper than just religion. Baigent et al. point out that the Catholic Church was desperate and needed political backing in order to survive; otherwise, heresy—the name Rome used for those who thought differently—threatened to exclude it.

Using the Queen's confessor, Rémy, who was later canonized just like Clotilde, they hatched a plan. Clotilde, lectured by the friar, made a proposal to the King that he convert to Catholicism under the following conditions: the Church would once again lead the religious roost and would have political power, and in return Clovis would be granted the title "Novus Constantinus." Described like that it does not seem to be much of a bargain, but in fact being the "New Constantine" amounted to making Clovis the legitimate heir of the Holy Roman Empire as was Constantine after his mysterious conversion. In other words, if we look closely, behind all the royal "visions" lies the Church negotiating in the background.

In the Battle of Vouillé in 507, Clovis defeated the Visigoths and expanded his realm right up to the Pyrenees. According to the theories that we have been analyzing, the Jews were in that region, as were Jesus' descendants who independently ruled the Kingdom of Septimania—including Nîmes, Narbonne and the Pyrenees—until the invasion of the Moors in the 8th century. That bloodline fused with the

Merovingian line at some indeterminate point during history, with the result that the descendants of the House of David had rights to the future French throne.

Following the death of Clovis in 511 other kings succeeded him, most notably Chlothar I. However, the drama surrounding this lineage was about to unfold, mainly due to the indolent attitude of the last monarchs, with the exception of Dagobert II.

Dagobert II was born in 651, but was kidnapped by Palace Mayor Grimoald, who maintained that the heir had died and maneuvred to occupy the position of power. However, he made the fatal mistake of keeping the child alive and confessed to the Bishop of Poitiers, who sent Dagobert to a monastery in Ireland. There he married a Celtic princess called Mathilde, who could only bear him daughters and died in 670 during her third birth.

Dagobert II returned to France and recovered the kingdom that had been taken from him. He remarried, this time Giselle of Razes, a region near Rennes-le-Château. It was here that Dagobert II set up his head-quarters with the hope of getting back the throne, which takes us back to Languedoc, not far from where this story allegedly took place.

He had two more daughters with his new wife and, finally, the long-awaited son and heir to the throne: Sigisbert. Nonetheless, his enemies, including the Church who he had controlled during his craving for power, and the noblemen represented by Palace Mayor Pippin of Heristal, were intent on his downfall.

According to the legend, one day the King was hunting in the Forest of Woevres when he suddenly felt tired. He lay down on a riverbank and while he was sleeping he was lanced through the eye by an assassin hired by Pippin. Afterwards, the wave of violence spread through the palace and the entire royal family was murdered. The entire family? That is the secret of the matter.

Generations on—and one or two Pippins later—Charles Martel started the Carolingian dynasty. By then it was the 8th century. But what would have happened if one of Dagobert II's children had survived?

The relics of Dagobert II have been the object of worship, and he was even canonized in 872—not by the Pope, but by a metropolitan church. Why? And why were battles fought to gain control of the church where it is alleged his body lies, in Stenay? Is it a coincidence

The Knights Templar, experts on this story, may have gone to great lengths to protect the secret and were consequently exterminated.

that the Duke of Lorraine granted this church special protection in 1069? And finally, is it a coincidence that the Duke of Lorraine was the grandfather of Godfrey of Bouillon—who we will introduce shortly— the first King of Jerusalem following the First Crusade?

According to these hair-raising theories that Dan Brown uses for his novel, Sigisbert did not die during the murder of the royal family. He was saved by Meroveus Levy, a surname that recalls the Jewish past of many important figures according to Lincoln et al. The heir to the throne was hidden in the same place where, years earlier, his father had waited for the right time to recover his kingdom: Rennes-le-Château.

The mythical character of the person known as Sigisbert IV was reflected by his nickname *Plant Ard,* which means "sapling." According to Gérard de Sède, after he married the daughter of the Visigoth King Wamba the bloodline of the Counts of Razès was started, followed years later by the Blancheforts, many of them linked to the Cathars and the Knights Templar.

This long story can be summed up as follows: the Merovingian bloodline, which did not die out, is the only one that should legitimately hold the French throne. Or going further back in time, the French throne would belong to the heirs of the *Sang Real.*

The plot thickens, and it turns out that one descendant of this bloodline was William of Gellone, one of the main Knights of Charlemagne or *Peers* and that, if this version is to be believed, he would be the son of the once Jewish king of Septimania, Theodoricus. William of Gellone was Count of Toulouse and of Razès, and carried Merovingian and Jewish blood in his veins. The authors of *The Messianic Legacy* claim that the device on his shield is the same as that of the Eastern 'exilarchs'—the Lion of Judah, the tribe to which the house of David and, subsequently, Jesus belonged.

The authors of this book quote Arthur Zuckerman, who points out that this medieval warrior passionately upheld Jewish customs: *"The chronicler who wrote the original report about the siege and fall of Barcelona reported the events in accordance with the Jewish calendar ... (The) leader of the expedition, Duke William of Narbonne and Toulouse, led the campaign strictly observing Saturdays and Jewish holy days. Throughout he received the understanding and cooperation of King Louis."*

The same authors maintain that when Louis was crowned king, William was the person who placed the crown on his head and, to everyone's surprise, the King said: *"Sir William...it is your lineage that has given rise to mine."*

It is said that this enigmatic man died in 806. By then, Gellone had a rabbinic academy and it was the site of a Mary Magdalene cult.

Wearing heavily rose-tinted glasses, these researchers boldly state that, in spite of the swings of history, branches of this mythical family spread through some important clans of medieval Christianity. These included the Dukes of Aquitaine during the 9th century and the House of Lorraine. As regards the latter, it is said that Hugues de Plantard, a descendant of the Grail Family, was the father of Eustache, the first Count of Boulougne, and grandfather of Godfrey of Bouillon, Duke of Lower Lorraine. At this point we will open the gates to Jerusalem wide, since the Crusades are just around the corner.

The Knights Templar

A FEW PARAGRAPHS EARLIER WE ARRIVED AT THE MIDDLE AGES after having sailed across one thousand years of history. Our bold ship cleaved the darkest seas and our faces were splashed with cold, terrifying water. Without giving us time to breathe, we are going to plunge into one of the most important conspiracies in the history of humanity, which is one of the parts of the great lie that some authors claim we have been forced to swallow for two thousand years.

The Holy Order of the Poor Knights of the Temple of Solomon, more commonly known as the Knights Templar, has sparked all kinds of speculations regarding the reason for its founding, its spectacular and sudden acquisition of wealth, and its dramatic and bloody end. It is impossible to sum up the whole story here, which ranges from the start of the 12th century until the dawn of the 14th century, including the Order's economic and political activities. To make the picture that we are painting for the reader a little clearer, we are only interested in its founding and objectives.

The official historiography, according to which this order is no different from the others that appeared in the East during the time of the First Crusade, does not give the exact time when it was founded. Authors such as Mestre admit that the date is uncertain, suggesting both the year 1118 and 1119. Nonetheless, they are more assured when they establish a date for the demise of the Knights Templar: March 22, 1312, when Pope Clement V dissolved the Order by Papal Bull after having been spurred on by the French King Phillip IV the Fair, who longed to acquire the riches of the Templars, to whom he owed huge amounts of money. To achieve this he invented false charges of sorcery, blasphemy, sodomy, and other similar accusations.

When speaking about the beginnings of this order, historians prefer to use the vague accounts written by William of Tyre and Jacques de Vitry. The former was Patriarch of Jerusalem, but was born in 1130 when the events that concern us had already taken place, which means that he had to use other sources or stories that he heard. Amalric I (1163-1174) was King at the time this author wrote *Historia rerum in partibus transmarinis gestarum*. The following is an extract from this book: *"In the same year [1118], certain noble men of knightly rank, devoted to God, pious and God-fearing, made a profession before the lord patriarch to live perpetually in chastity and obedience and without property, in the manner of the regular canons, giving themselves up to the service of Christ. The first and foremost among them were the venerable men Hugh of Payns and Godfrey of St. Omer."*

The other aforementioned chronicler, Jacques de Vitry, wrote *Historia Orientalis seu Hierosolymitana*. This author was Bishop of Acre in the 12th century, and wrote: *"Certain noble men of knightly rank devoted to God and ordained for His service gave themselves up to serve Christ (...) The leaders were the venerable men Hugh of Payns and Godfrey of St. Omer. At first only nine took this holy decision and, for nine years, they dressed in secular clothing which the faithful gave to them as charity (...). And since they did not have a church or a place to live the King gave them shelter in his palace, near the Lord's Temple, (...) for this reason they came to be called 'Knights Templar.'"*

Both quotations were written a long while after the events happened. Nor do we have archives that can prove these versions, as Alain Demurger admits: *"almost all of them are donations, they do not explain the Templar origins."*

In spite of this, the version accepted by orthodox historians claims that the events happened in this way and that for nine years there were nine knights in Jerusalem who protected the pilgrims who arrived at the Holy Land. The driving force behind the group and the leader was a noble Frenchman called Hugh of Payns. In order to better understand the context, we should now briefly describe the Crusades.

We have mentioned that this enigmatic group of French and Flemish origin supposedly arrived in Jerusalem in 1118. We should point out that years earlier, on November 27, 1095, Pope Urban II harangued Christians at the Council of Clermont to recover the Holy Land, which was under the control of the infidels, according to their religious view of matters.

Official historians believe that there were different objectives behind this proposal: financial—starting trading in the Mediterranean; political—the Pope acquired a powerful army, even more powerful than those of many kings; and religious—everyone who participated in the Crusade was forgiven. With that privilege of popes who know what God thinks and wants, Urban II stirred up the spirits and, declaring that it was God's will, urged the people to wear a cross and march in pursuit of glory. Of course, there is no evidence that he himself came face to face with a Saracen in the middle of the desert. But the fact is that he achieved success and his ideas have had many followers.

Indeed, while the Pope's military mission was being organized, a person called Peter the Hermit lived in France. He was a dazzlingly articulate man said to be the private tutor of some of the key players in this mission. Peter rode from one place to another on a mule and managed to gather hundreds of persons enthralled by his sermons, who went forth to the Holy Land ahead of the real soldiers. They were armed with courage but only carried scythes and sticks. Predictably, in Civitot, Asia Minor, the infidels put them to the sword and left hardly any of them alive, when suddenly bugles sounded in the distance and a cloud of dust rose skywards. Who were they? They were the real soldiers, armed to the teeth. They were God's soldiers.

Imagine the scene: thousands of men drunk on religion, who really believe what the Pope told them, take Jerusalem on July 14, 1099 and lay waste to everything and everyone in their path.

And the crusaders marched forth to Jerusalem, ready to die for the Holy Land.

"The city was the site of a massacre of the enemies, and there was such blood-shed that even the victors were filled with horror and dread," wrote William of Tyre. The Latin Kingdom of Jerusalem was built on top of thousands of corpses, and extended from Lebanon to the Sinai by sheer force.

Godfrey of Bouillon was offered the position of King, but all of a sudden he was gripped by an attack of humility and declared, we suppose to everyone's surprise, that he thought it not appropriate to wear a royal crown where Jesus had worn a crown of thorns, and he consented to be called the Defender of the Holy Sepulchre. When he died in 1100, his brother Baldwin was not averse to wearing the crown and donned it without further ado. Thus, Baldwin I became king.

Meanwhile, the people set about organizing themselves. In 1110 The Order of the Hospital of Saint John of Jerusalem came into being, followed a couple of years later by the Order of Teutonic Knights. Further along the line, in 1118, arrived the nine enigmatic knights led by Hugh of Payns and the beginnings of the Templar Order. By then, King Baldwin I had been replaced by Baldwin II.

After a nine-year stay in Jerusalem, with no historical record of having participated in any battles, skirmishes, quarrels, or fights in the name of protecting either pilgrims or God, Hugh of Payns and five of his knights returned to France. Only three stayed behind to defend we know not what. And when we say that for nine years there were only nine of them, it is not just because we feel like saying it or to be annoying. Indeed, we are using the exact words of William of Tyre: *"Although the knights now had been established for nine years, there were still only nine of them."* Of course, Demurger claims that this statement is false and that there must have been more of them, but he has not been able to provide any evidence to back his theory. If official historians do not doubt William of Tyre when he states that nine knights led by Hugh of Payns founded the Templar Order, then they must also accept the rest of this chronicler's claims and not just keep those that best fit in with their academic way of thinking.

Furthermore, why did they go to France after stopping first in Rome? Well, there they received Papal recognition and were given a proper Rule. This Rule was granted in 1128 at the Council of Troyes in Champagne and was written by Cistercian abbot Bernard of

Clairvaux, who bore the torch of Christianity in those times and was the nephew of one of the nine mythical Knights Templar, Andrew of Montbard.

However, what does Demurger have to say about this journey? He maintains that Hugh of Payns' travels around France from that time onwards occured because the Order was suffering a growth crisis. In his opinion, the knight was looking for followers. But, does the same source not claim that there were more than nine of them at that stage? He specifically says that *"the Knights Templar were a much larger group."* In other words, we are faced with strange contradictions. The most significant in our opinion is the claim that the group was joined by a tenth person, the Count of Champagne and also called Hugh, in 1125, after disowning his wife and transferring all of his land to his nephew, Thibaud of Blois.

A recap of the mysteries

IF THE READER HAS THE PATIENCE required to read just a few pages more on this topic, they will understand what these events have to do with the tangled web contained in *The Da Vinci Code*. To make this easier, we will sum up some of the main points regarding the Knights Templar.

The authors of the book *The Templars and the Lost Word* show their disagreement with the official versions of this historical event. It is true that our version differs from that which novelist Dan Brown and other aforementioned authors use, but these ideas do agree on some points that we will briefly study below.

It certainly seems odd that a group of strangers, even if they were nine knights, appeared before Baldwin II, King of Jerusalem, and with no credentials other than their faith, were granted use of the latter's official place of residence which was where the Temple of Jerusalem, built by Solomon and later rebuilt by Herod, used to stand.

This story is harder to believe if we add that the group's "ideologist" was apparently a dark knight and French nobleman called Hugh of Payns, a town in Champagne next to Troyes, where the Order was granted their Rule.

Even more mysterious is the fact that the King ended up granting them the entire Temple site, including the mosques there at the time. This site was formed by one small octagonal area called Kubbat-el-Silsileh or the Dome of the Chain, another grand one called Kubbat-el-Sakhra or the Dome of the Rock, and another called Kubbat-el-Aqsa.

We must also add to this strange situation the fact that for nine years these people did not once leave the premises, a magic holy place. It was from there that Mohammed had ascended to heaven on his inimitable mule; it was there that Abraham proved his faith in Jehovah and almost sacrificed his son Isaac; it was there that Jehovah placed the center of the world; and it was there that the Temple of Solomon was built. The

Templar castle in Ponferrada, the great Spanish fortress.

question we have to ask is: what were those nine mysterious knights doing there? Furthermore, no less shocking is the fact that Hugh of Champagne, Count of the region and Hugh of Payns' lord, joined the group in 1125 and bowed to the orders of his vassal, something quite impossible if we consider the strict social structure of the Middle Ages.

Finally, we must mention two coincidences that happen shortly afterwards: the astronomical wealth of the Templars and their sudden presence in Gothic cathedrals around Europe, which are especially abundant in France.

Some answers

THE AFOREMENTIONED BOOK ATTEMPTS TO provide a global solution to this intricate plot, but we will now move slightly away from this theory to explain the basis of the "Da Vinci argument" and the opinions that we have put forward up until now. Let us see if it works.

The first thing to point out is that there is historical evidence that Hugh of Champagne travelled to the Holy Land years before the famous knights. According to Charpentier, the aforementioned nobleman, who was a lord in the regions where almost all the following events occurred, was in Jerusalem, *"it is not known exactly when, but it is generally established between 1104 and 1105."* In other words, fourteen years before the mission led by Hugh of Payns. In addition, it would appear that he returned to Jerusalem in 1108. In that case, he made two journeys. Why?

Our personal interpretation is linked to Stephen Harding, the second abbot of the Cistercian Order. He may have sent Hugh of Payns with a specific mission due to the discovery of something highly significant that had appeared in some manuscripts. Jewish rabbis from Champagne, paid by the Order, worked on these manuscripts, among whom the mythical Rashi of Troyes was probably present. The story that we are going to consider here is rather different from our idea.

Nonetheless, the fact remains important: Hugh of Champagne travelled to Jerusalem twice, years before the appearance of the first Knights Templar.

Secondly, Hugh of Champagne assigned land in Clairvaux to the Cistercian Order. This was required for founding a monastery to be run by Bernard, the soul of the future Templar Order, since it was he who oversaw their Rule.

Bernard of Clairvaux and Hugh of Champagne appear to be friends, as evidenced in the following letter sent by the abbot to the nobleman and reproduced by Michel Lamy: *"If, for God's work, you have changed yourself from count to knight and from rich to poor, we congratulate you and glorify God in you, knowing that this is a change in the name of the Lord's cause. I must confess that we are sad to have your joyful presence taken away from us for God's justice, which justice I do not know, unless we are granted the privilege of seeing you from time to time, if possible, which we desire more than anything."*

Clearly the two men felt a great affection for each other. But there is more. The names of the first nine knights were: Andrew of Montbard, Godfrey of Saint-Omer, Payen of Montdidier and Archembaud of Saint-Amand, Gondemar, Godfrey, Rossal, and Godfrey Bisol. Now, the first of these men was the uncle of Bernard of Clairvaux and, like the two knights mentioned below, was part of the entourage of Eustache of Boulogne, the brother of Godfrey of Bouillon, who we said earlier refused to wear the crown after the First Crusade.

Therefore, they seem to be woven into the same plot. Furthermore, if these knights were part of an entourage close to the family of Godfrey of Bouillon then it is not strange that Baldwin II offered them lodging in his palace, as they were not strangers. However, it is still odd that he should have given them all of the buildings on the site of the Temple, unless not only did he know them, but he was afraid of them or he had a duty to them.

Let us continue briefly with Champagne, the region ruled by Hugh. We still find it strange that Payns was one of the fiefs under his command; that Troyes, where the Council that granted the Templar Order its Rule took place, was on his land; that today there are still places that bear witness to the Order—land grants, Templar Lake, Templar Forest; that Pope Urban II, who preached the First Crusade, was from Champagne...and that there are legends, echoed by authors such as Charpentier, according to which the Knights Templar made a mysterious discovery right there at the heart of the ancient site of King Solomon's Temple.

Does this accumulation of coincidences not seem odd?

The reader might be wondering why the story has taken a sudden turn. Were we not tracing the possible existence of Jesus' lineage? What has that got to do with the Knights Templar?

Jacques de Molay and Geoffrey de Charney are executed in Paris. This is the end of the Templar Order.

We decided to deal with the Templar Order first because the mysteries surrounding it are well-known. Also, we wanted to warn the reader about the clear contradictions of the conventional version of its founding. We have not touched upon other possible solutions, which fascinate us so much that we have dedicated books and several years of research to the topic.

The Priory of Sion

IN THE NOVEL THAT GIVES US AN EXCUSE TO TREAD along the paths towards heresy, the main character, Langdon, tells Sophie, the other main character, about a secret society called the Priory of Sion. What does this have to do with the Knights Templar and Jesus' alleged lineage? In fact a great deal, as we will soon see. Langdon says that: *"The Priory of Sion was founded in Jerusalem in 1099 by a French king named Godefroi of Bouillon, immediately after he had conquered the city."* And the reason why it was founded? Langdon's reply to our question is: *"King Godefroi was allegedly the possessor of a powerful secret—a secret that had been in his family since the time of Christ."*

We can now see a series of links between all of the paths that we have covered until now, since in these statements there are references to Jesus Christ, a secret, Godfrey of Bouillon, the capture of Jerusalem, and a new, secret society called the Priory of Sion. Next we will attempt to tie up all the loose ends to give the reader a full picture.

Earlier we mentioned the theories held by different authors who claim that the Merovingian descendants, allegedly related to those of Christ at some vague point in history, mixed with different medieval houses of nobility. We mentioned the importance of the House of Lorraine and how the members of the latter showed a strange interest in the church where Dagobert II, the murdered Merovingian King, was buried. We even referred to Eustache, the first Count of Boulogne, who played an important role in those incidents and who was the grandfather of Godfrey of Bouillon.

Thus, if we choose to believe this theory, Godfrey's family was related to the mythical Holy Grail bloodline. The House of Lorraine that Godfrey represented would therefore be linked to this bloodline. To the causes that we mentioned for the First Crusade—economic, political and religious—we should perhaps add another of a mysterious or initiatory nature, but no less political: Godfrey represented Jesus of Nazareth's bloodline, i.e. the lineage of David. And when he conquered Jerusalem the circle was closed. It could be said that the *Holy Blood* was going home.

The authors of *Holy Blood, Holy Grail* say that in the 16th century Henry of Lorraine, at that time Duke of Guise, upon entering the town of Joinville in Champagne was received by exuberant crowds. Among them certain individuals are reported to have chanted, "Hosannah, filio David!"—Hosannah to the son of David!

This extraordinary news, shocking due to its reckless implications for history, is not the only surprise in store. Let us see where this line leads that we have traced regarding the Templar Order.

As we have seen, there are many mysteries surrounding the time when the Knights Templar were founded, as well as their real purpose. We have discovered some clues, but we did leave one path open which we will now pick up and this directly links Godfrey of Bouillon to the Knights Templar.

At the end of the 1950s and beginning of the 1960s, a group of documents began to make their way around Europe which had been kept secret up until then. We will say more about these below, but for now we will mention one relevant basic fact: those documents speak about a secret society founded by Godfrey of Bouillon. This mysterious group called themselves the Order of Sion.

The controversial manuscripts stated that the family of Baldwin I, who succeeded Godfrey as King of Jerusalem, was royal *jure sanguinis*. Also, Godfrey of Bouillon had founded this mysterious Order nine years before the Crusades took Jerusalem—some authors claim that it was founded in 1090; others in 1099. They go on to claim that Baldwin I was king thanks to that society, which apparently had its headquarters in the Abbey of Notre Dame du Mont de Sion, Jerusalem.

As far as we know, chronicles about the Crusades do not mention this group, which does not invalidate the possibility of its existence if its purpose was to be discrete and guard a dangerous secret. However, there does seem to have been an old Byzantine church on Mount Zion, where the famous abbey was built on Godefroi's initiative. This site must have drawn a lot of attention given that it was fortified by walls and battlements.

Baigent et al. declare that *"the knights and monks who occupied the Church of the Holy Sepulchre, also built by Godefroi, were formed into an official and duly constituted 'order,' specifically, the Order of the Holy Sepulchre,"* and they conclude that a very similar event happened at the church on Mount Zion, i.e., an order was founded there. To confirm their suspicions, they quote M. de Vogüé in his book entitled *Les Eglises de la Terre Sainte*. This claims that that community existed and was called Saint Mary of Mount Sion and of the Holy Spirit. Moving on...

The above is explained even more clearly in Vincent's book *Histoire de l'Ancienne Image Miraculeuse de Notre Dame de Sion*, in which the following was written in 1968: *"In Jerusalem during the crusades ... knights joined the Abbey of Notre Dame who adopted the name Chevaliers de l'Ordre de Notre Dame de Sion."*

Therefore, years before the future Knights Templar arrived on the scene, there was already a mysterious order inspired by Godfrey of Bouillon. We have also seen that Hugh of Champagne travelled to Jerusalem before the Knights made themselves known in public. Also, we have pointed out that some of those first nine warrior monks were part of Godefroi's brother's entourage and that many of these persons were friends or had family ties. But now we will continue with this heresy from a religious and historical point of view.

The Priory and the Knights Templar

HISTORIAN JOSÉ ÁNGEL GARCÍA DE CORTAZAR identifies the importance of two movements prior to the monastic adventures in the West during medieval times. He refers to the important activity of monks in Southern Italy, especially in Apulia and Calabria, who he claims held *"Egyptian, Greek, and Byzantine traditions."* It is said that in 1070, twenty-nine years before Jerusalem was taken during the First Crusade, a specific band of monks from Calabria arrived in the vicinity of the Ardennes Forest, coincidentally part of Godfrey of Bouillon's domains.

According to French writer Gérard de Sède, this band of monks was led by an individual called Ursus, a name associated with the Merovingian bloodline. The monks obtained the patronage of Mathilde de Toscan, Godfrey of Bouillon's aunt and, in effect, foster mother. They received a tract of land at Orval, where they built an abbey. Yet another coincidence: this was not far from Stenay, where Merovingian King Dagobert II had been assassinated.

By the early years of the 12th century there was no trace of these monks, who it is said included the mythical Peter the Hermit, the man who we have seen spurred on a crusade of fanatical Christians before the official crusade called by the Pope. It is also said that he was Godfrey of Bouillon's private tutor. Is this sufficient reason to think that the monks knew something important about the royal bloodline and alerted Godfrey? Can we begin to think that these secrets led to the idea of recovering the holy places to perharps take something that proved King David's lineage? Was the purpose perhaps to recovery of those abovementioned documents that might have been buried in the heart of the site of Solomon's Temple?

Of course, these are just speculations, although some authors strive to prove the foundations of this theory, which does indeed have an alluring air about it. The fact remains that many names and pieces start to suddenly fit together: the unexpected idea of the Crusade, the presence of Godfroi de Bouillon in the leading role, the journeys made by Hugh of Champagne before his vassal Hugo de Payns arrived in Jerusalem with eight companions, many of them friends, acquaintances or relatives...

We have just referred to the existence of some curious documents that appeared in the 20th century which mention the Priory of Sion. Some of these, the so-called *Dossiers Secrets*, also speak about the Templar Order and its founders. They mention the following: *"Hugues de Payen, Bisol de St. Omer and Hugues, Count of Champagne, along with some members of the Order of Sion, André de Montbard, Archambaud de Saint-Aignan, Nivard de Montdidier, Gondemar and Rossal."*

"The Shepherds of Arcadia" by Nicolas Poussin, a mysterious painting that contains clues as to Christ's possible bloodline.

What should surprise us is that André de Montbard, uncle of Bernard de Clairvaux, is mentioned not only as one of the founders of the Templar Order but as a member of the mysterious Order of Sion. Therefore, it is clear that the latter did exist and was around before the founding of the Templar Order, to the delight of those who support this complicated theory.

The same source states that in March 1117 King Baldwin I, *"who owed the Sion the crown,"* was *"forced"* to negotiate the founding of the Templar Order. In other words, this would explain why the monarch granted the buildings on the site of the Temple and his own palace to a group of newcomers. He did not know them, but was forced to do so by orders of the Order of Sion, to whom he owed the throne.

The same current of opinion claims that the Knights Templar, who we suspect had been founded earlier—or had come from another, older secret group—was the military arm of the Order of Sion. Meanwhile, the Abbey in Orval where the Calabrian monks had settled was taken over by Bernard of Claraval. As you can see, the plot does not leave any loose ends.

For many years, until 1188, the Grand Masters of the Knights Templar and of the Order of Sion were the same persons, according to the secret manuscripts—which of course did not stay secret. It is said that in 1152, during the reign of the French King Louis VII, ninety-five members of the Order returned to France and set up their Grand Priory in Orléans. Baigent, Lincoln, and Leigh claim to have found evidence of the latter in municipal archives, which even include a papal bull passed in 1178 by Pope Alexander III which officially confirms the property owned by this Order in Orléans. However, suddenly both mysterious Orders, the Knights Templar and the Order of Sion, split in 1188 for reasons that are not yet clear. One year later Jerusalem had fallen to the Muslims and the story goes that Gérard de Ridefort, Grand Master of the Knights Templar, was closely linked to this military disaster. The aforementioned *Dossiers Secrets* state that he committed treason, but this is not at all clear. The members of the Order of Sion returned to France and something must have happened in Gisors to cause the splitting of both societies. There is still something that we do not fully understand: if they both had the same Grand Master, why would the Order of Sion accuse the Master of the Knights Templar of treason?

Whatever the case, near the castle of Gisors, which was owned by the Templars, there was a field called the "Holy Field" where there was a thousand-year-old elm tree so large that a ring of nine men could not encircle it. Something happened there, although exactly what is not known.

Some medieval chronicles mention a clash between the French and English kings and their respective men, although this would not have anything to do with the characters of our story. Nevertheless, if we are to believe the famous *Dossiers Secrets*, it was there that the Order of Sion and the Knights Templar split and this was represented by the felling of the thousand-year-old elm tree.

From that moment onwards, each order went its own way and had their own Grand Masters. The Order of Sion changed its name to the Priory of Sion. The Knights Templar continued to increase their power, wealth, and perhaps secret knowledge. But was this the same secret knowledge that the Priory of Sion managed to hide so well? Why did the Priory almost literally disappear? Maybe due to the great secret that it kept, explained as follows by Langdon in *The Da Vinci Code*: "...During their years in Jerusalem, the Priory learned of a stash of hidden documents buried beneath the ruins of Herod's temple (...) These documents, they believed, corroborated Godefroi's powerful secret and were so explosive in nature that the Church would stop at nothing to get them."

The Church would kill for them—Montsegur

MONTSEGUR WAS UP THERE, on the summit of a mountain that looked impossible to get to, but which, with a hearty effort, could be reached. But it was up there broken, like an old toy. It was dead, barren, uninhabited, parched like the divine side of man. And the saddest thing of all? It was the Church, in the name of God, that devastated Montsegur.

Montsegur fortress, inside which a great treasure was kept...

Why?

The first thing that we want to point out is that we are in the heart of the Languedoc region, in southeast France. In other words, opposite that region where the belief was spread that Mary Magdalene landed carrying the Holy Grail. We are on the border with those first sanctuaries in memory of Our Lady holding infant Horus in her arms. The land where the Black Virgins spread like an epidemic. A strange region was Languedoc, which had its own language and where there was a religious tolerance similar to that enjoyed in Al-Andalus for a few centuries. Mountains and valleys where culture thrived beyond expectations and which for a while was not part of the Kingdom of France. A handful of noble families, the most important being the House of

Trencavel, ruled that region, to which the Church brought its religion shouting, while foaming at the mouth, that the region was infected by *"the foul leprosy of the south."*

As we look up to Montsegur we can be sure to see one of the faces of God, thinking that we would have been pleased to have suffered from that leprosy.

If we had had sufficient memory in those days, the following words written by Juan Eslava Galán would have sprung to mind: *"Circa 1150, a group of curious bearded missionaries appeared in the Languedoc region in Southern France. They usually travelled in pairs, dressed in black or dark blue and wore a rope belt. They preached to the humble in squares and marketplaces, in villages and cities, but they did not avoid the mansions of some noblemen or wealthy merchants..."*

...exactly the same as Jesus, who some people reproached for approaching publicans, gentiles, and other people who appeared sinful in the eyes of an orthodox Jew. Where did those mysterious men appear from?

According to the most widely held version, in the 10th century a movement appeared in the Bulgaria region called the *Bogomils* whose main objective was to upset the Church, maintaining that they were on the side of the "White God" or spirit of good, in the struggle with the "Black God," the spirit of evil.

This first overview should be alarming since the ancient Gnostics, those who believed in a God without any religious go-betweens and whose ideas were similar to those of the early Christians, also believed in forces that represented Good and others that represented Evil. Being the dreamers that we are, we ask ourselves whether this could be linked to the traditional Templar battle flag called the *Beauséant* which was precisely black and white?

These men and women were later called *cathari*, from the Greek *katharos* meaning "pure." This is thus how these unusual preachers came to be called "the pure ones" or "the good men" (in the local dialect, "parfaits").

The ideas that they preached spread like wildfire in that region, especially in cities like Albi, where their first Bishop came from, recalls Mestre. When the Church realized what was at stake and decided to ask God directly—only the Church has the right to do so—what should be done, they ended up pejoratively calling these people "Albigenses."

Strangely enough, this region was brimming with the Holy Grail history and there were Knights Templar waiting around every corner. Meanwhile, the noblemen welcomed the new ideas so enthusiastically that we are inclined to think that this was because they fit in, like an exact replica, with the age-old philosophies that dated back to at least the time when Mary Magdalene arrived in the south of France.

Historians such as Julio Valdeón point out the strange success of this deviation from official Christianity quite unlike other so-called heresies: *"...unlike what had occurred with the ancient Eastern heresies, which had only really affected the clergy, the Waldensian movement and above all Catharism, aroused a great deal of interest among the people."*

Why did this happen? What did the Cathars say that was accepted by the humblest farmer or the most intellectually challenged miller? Why did these ideas captivate the poor and rich alike? What sparked the Church's fury? Is it a coincidence that their other main headquarters was in Champagne, the region where the Templars were founded?

We should point out that the people were tired of a Church that did not practice what it preached, that demanded exorbitant tithes from the humblest of workers, and only knew how to churn out the well-worn argument of sinning and eternal hell.

It was at this point that a group of men and women arrived on the scene who did not speak pompously, whose habits were humble and did not contain bellies full from feast and merrymaking, and who did not believe in hell. According to them, man achieves perfection in his final incarnation that permits him to fuse with the good God.

The preachers spoke of poverty and set an example. They declared they were against all kinds of violence, including that directed towards animals. They looked after their bodies meticulously, which is why they did not eat eggs or milk but did eat fish.

They rejected the Old Testament and preached in pairs, gathering in public houses run by elderly persons in which men and women had the same say and held the same amount of control. Although all of the above irked the Church, it was the last two that really stung—seeing

Stone plaque in honor of the terrible massacre of Cathars at Montsegur. But the "treasure" was already safe...

women playing an important role brings the Church straight out in a rash. What were women doing officiating at rites? What was all that about walking around preaching as if they knew what they were talking about? Did they not take a long time to decide whether females had a soul or not? How could they teach lessons to anyone?

But there was more behind all this hatred. There was the Church's ancient precaution towards anything that reminded them of the old cult at which priestesses officiated. Indeed, they were just a step away from reviving the fertility represented by Isis, Astarte, Venus, and—heaven forbid!—Mary Magdalene.

The Cathars believed in an eternal battle between these two principles of light and darkness, with man representing the swords brandished by invisible hands. Both principles are eternal. Good equals things spiritual and Evil things material. Therefore, no matter can be pure, not even man, or even Jesus, since He became incarnate on Earth.

In our opinion, those people were cruelly attacked by the Church for two main reasons: because of those two philosophical principles that we have stressed, which included rites whose nature we do not know, and because of some treasure that they possessed. The much-discussed Cathar rites included the mysterious *Consolamentum* ceremony, which, like other ancient initiation rites, was a mixture of public and private. The public part could be compared to the ordination of Catholic priests, and the private was like a magic show with the laying on of hands during which the subject underwent some kind of transformation. According to Michel Lamy, through this rite the Cathars *"believed that man was given back his divine soul."*

In *The Templars and the Lost Word*, this ceremony is analyzed in great detail, and the authors agree with the idea proposed by Maurice Magre regarding the *Consolamentum* that this was *"Christ's secret, the spirit of the Holy Grail. "* However, we will go no further along this path that we have followed in search of the mysterious Knights Templar, although we will use it briefly for our mission at hand. The fact is that there seem to be links between the Cathar doctrine, the secret of the Knights Templar, and the possible nature of the Holy Grail.

We are sure that the reader will agree that all of these affairs were too dangerous for the Church. A fine thing it would be if man decided to look for God on his own! That's going a bit far!

These would undoubtedly be good reasons for the black cassocks to bring the cruel God of the Old Testament out from the closet, the God that they always have on hand when there is a need to kill anyone who does not have the same beliefs. It is possible that the undue hatred that led to the events taking place up at Montsegur was caused by something far more serious, something terrible for the Church. If this was not these people's philosophy, then there must have been another motive: the Cathar treasure.

Pope Innocent III—what an ironic name!—began to count how many tithes and how many faithful—he probably counted in that order—the Church was losing in Languedoc, concluding a lot, even too many. So, glancing briefly at God, who the Pope can always consult, he decided to go to war. Or rather, the Crusade. We must mention that these shameless people, who use and abuse God's name to their advantage, called the campaign the "Albigensian Crusade." It basically consisted of killing Christians, but *the other* Christians, those who held different beliefs. Participants were promised eternal salvation and everything else included in the whole package usually offered when Catholics go to battle in the name of God.

And so, thirsty for land and gushing over the possibility of possessing the Cathar treasure, in 1209 the Pope's men arranged to meet in Lyons. Those who saw them said that there were around twenty thousand cavalrymen and twice as many infantrymen.

The crusade was a massacre. The Cathars were few and the local nobles who protected them could hardly compete with the Pope's mass of men. They began to fall, one by one and then thousand by thousand. Finally, the city of Béziers was reached.

It was July 22. The troops representing God were under the command of a man whose name stills strikes terror in Languedoc today.

This man was Simon of Montfor. Regarding the civilians in Béziers, he said to his men *"slay them all, for God will recognise which are His."* But maybe God was weeping and could not make anyone out through His tears. Maybe He was tired of the whole affair and had become a Cathar.

Once Languedoc was a bloodbath and the fields begged for mercy under the hooves of the Pope's horses, only one place was still standing. That place was the fortress in ruins where that eve we thought we saw the sorrowful fate of the divine side of humans: Montsegur.

Up there, sheltered by a massif called Tabe—similar to Tabor, where some say Jesus' Transfiguration took place—and looking down over the valley from the proud height of 1,272 meters were the Cathars, guardians of the treasure.

This fortress had been built at the orders of Raymond of Blasco between 1205 and 1211, and seems to have been designed on the site of an ancient temple, in keeping with its magical nature.

There was no way of taking the fortress by storm, at least not for the time being, thought the Church's army. Therefore, they laid siege to it. And the siege carried on. Supplies were sent to the castle by locals who knew how to get around the besiegers.

Some researchers maintain that three months before the end, in January, two "parfaits" sneaked out carrying all the treasures they could that were kept in the fortress. Nobody saw them; it is all just a legend. At the beginning of March it was decided to take the fortress by storm. There were fewer than four thousand people inside, and at least two hundred were "parfaits." In the end they surrendered. The Church was oddly lenient, perhaps thinking that the treasure was within reach. Those who surrendered were required to confess their sins in order to be forgiven, otherwise they would be burned at the stake.

The Lord of the fortress, Raymond de Pereille, and his men negotiated the surrender of the castle to be allowed to stay there until March 16, 1244. Why until that date? Unfortunately, we may never know. However, according to legends, on the eve of that fateful day four

Cathars escaped, taking with them what many authors suspect was the real Cathar treasure. The same treasure that the Church tirelessly searched for the following day. Could this be the same that was hunted years later in the Templar's Tower in Paris, also in vain? On the following day, to the surprise of the besiegers, those who surrendered did not confess their sins and, in a shockingly disciplined line, were taken to huge improvised stakes in the field next to the castle, today known as *Camp dels Cremats*.

Goodbye, Holy Grail

WHAT DID THOSE FOUR CATHARS hide in their tunics or in a sack of unknown weight and length? What is known about them? To tell the truth, nothing specific. Tradition has it that one of them was called Amiel Alicart, another Hugues, and a third Pichel de Poitevin. In reality we are not interested in their names, but their reasons for waiting until the last day to commit the deed. Why did the truce have to last until March 16? Did a ceremony take place there that could only be held on that day and for which the Cathar treasure was needed? Maybe that is why they did not take it to safety earlier?

But of what could this treasure have consisted? Dusty parchments or chalices containing the blood of Christ? The Ark of the Covenant or, perhaps, the *Holy Blood* carried by the descendants of the bloodline whom the Church intended to assassinate once more, just like in the old times of Dagobert II? Who can provide the answers to any of these questions? There will be a reward for anyone who can...

Meanwhile researchers go on researching, which is what they are there for.

In the 1930s the Nazis entrusted the quest for the evasive Grail to Otto Rahn, a member of the SS, who is always mentioned in these chronicles. Others have conducted research on even more recent dates.

In the neighboring region of Sabarthes, Jean Blum discovered, to people's great shock, that deep in the Teille Forest there is a refuge called "of the Grail," and that in the entire region there are traces of the Grail past. We have worn out the soles of our boots in the cave of Lombrives trying to find the real track of the ancient Cathar treasure.

As it happens, it was during the times when the Cathar doctrine was being disseminated—and also at the peak of the Templar craze—when the never-ending story of the Holy Grail began to circulate around Europe. It is a suspicious coincidence that the first person to tell the mythical tale was a resident of Troyes, in the Templar land of Champagne. We are referring to Chrétien de Troyes.

This book was left unfinished, but other authors added the details and improvements that we all know so well. Two important editors were Robert de Boron and Wolfram von Eschenbach, who around 1210 clarified a few points, much to the excitement of the Cathar treasure hunters.

High up, the impregnable Montsegur fortress, where the genocide took place.

In Eschenbach's book *Parzival*, he states that the long-sought Holy Grail lies in a castle called *Muntsalvache* and that its faithful defenders are some members of the Knights Templar. Whether arrogance on his part or a severe attack of honesty we do not know, but he claims that his version, rather than the previous ones, is the authentic one. He reveals that one Kyot de Provence was his confidante and that in turn the latter had been told the story by a Jewish descendant of the Solomon bloodline called Flegetanis.

Some of these secrets are really quite juicy. Firstly, and we are going to believe Eschenbach here, we are told that the Knights Templar are explicitly involved in the Grail affair; secondly, the place where the blessed chalice or whatever is hidden in the shadows is a fortress with its own name, which is quite a historical breakthrough; and thirdly, all of these facts are told by someone from Provence—where Mary Magdalene landed—who in turn was informed by a descendent of King Solomon, that is, also from the House of David.

Researchers—who, we have said, are there to research—work hard and claim they can see an undeniable phonetic similarity between *Muntsalvache* from the Grail story and Cathar *Montsegur*. They thus tie up some loose ends. Furthermore, there is the treasure that no one ever found. Could this be the Holy Grail?

In *Parzival* mention is made of the Knights Templar, not the Cathars, as guardians. Nevertheless, we can draw some links between the two, and without being able to state that the Templars were Cathars, nor indeed to deny it, we can say that many Cathars were given a warm welcome on Templar-owned lands, which were abundant in the Languedoc region. Authors such as Dom Gérard have written that *"The Templar Order was at the core of the Cathar doctrine and of its spreading among the humble people and among the Occitan lords."*

Finally, let us consider Eschenbach's enigmatic reference to someone from Provence—Kyot—and a Jewish descendent of King Solomon as the guardian of the Grail tradition. Why does a Jew tell a story about

Christ when we all know that Jesus was never approved by the nation which considers itself to be the sons of Abraham? It does not seem to make an awful lot of sense, except that this Jew was a "descendent of King Solomon," and would therefore be linked to Jesus in that they are relations from the same House of David.

Does Eschenbach use a clever metaphor when he speaks about the *Holy Blood*? Unfortunately, we do not how to answer our own questions.

The Holy Grail, the *Sang Real* or whatever else is might be, bid us a farewell…or a "see you soon." Where was it hidden? There is talk of caves, grottos, forests. Could the four Cathars have gone very far when they sneaked out of Montsegur in the dark of night?

The caves of Sabarthes where the Cathars hid with their treasure.

That evening, while we thought we could hear the screams from the burnings at the stake, we suddenly remembered where we had come from and we thought that we might have travelled the same path as those four Cathars but the other way round. Indeed, a couple of hours earlier we had left behind Rennes-le-Château, where there was a priest that called Bethany home, and where the church is dedicated to Mary Magdalene...

Truth
Seekers

"Religion's in the heart, not in the knees..."

D. JERROLD

HOWEVER, WE WILL NOT YET TACKLE THE STEEP CLIMB that leads to the small town of Rennes, and which plunges us into a tangled web of streets where stone dominates and the smell of burning fills the air. Firstly, we must stop, even if for just a couple of paragraphs of this chapter, at the end of the 15th century when a genius of art and science is creating a painting, one of the most beautiful in the history of man... and also the most heavily laden with symbolism. This artist is Leonardo da Vinci, an obsessively inquisitive and highly talented man.

Leonardo was born in 1452 in Vinci, near Florence, the illegitimate son of notary public Ser Piero and a humble peasant woman from Tuscany. It goes without saying that he was one of the most phenomenal minds that humanity has ever known, during a time when the Renaissance of art and science boosted the intellectual development of a unique man.

A self-taught person in the broadest sense of the word, he was educated by his father. However, his natural talent soon shone through, creating superb works that were way ahead of his time. At the age of 16 he joined the studio of Andrea del Verocchio where he began to boldly produce unusual sketches. The fact is that Da Vinci was gifted, since no one has ever built up such encyclopedic knowledge that covered the most varied and diverse disciplines.

As could be expected, his interest in esoterism and occultism went beyond the imaginable; in short, in this field he also gained knowledge more arcane and momentous than any other. This is why many of his works are so highly charged with symbolism, and why there are few doubts that Da Vinci manipulated privileged information known by few ...and which resulted in many scholars being burned at the stake.

At the end of the year of the discovery of America, he was hired by the Duke of Milan, Ludovico Sforza. It must have been in that era when the mature Leonardo began to rub shoulders with all kinds of people, some of whom belonged to ancient societies that today we would call "secret". It was his most inspirational moment, since with boundless creativity he reached the peak of his skill, creating artistic and architectural works that are still admired all around the world.

In 1495, Ludovico "the Moor" commissioned Da Vinci to paint what became his most famous painting: "The Last Supper." This masterly fresco was finally placed in the refectory of the Convent of Santa María Delle Grazie, which the aforementioned duke wanted to turn into a private chapel for the Sforza Family. Chroniclers claim that two years of hard work saw Leonardo sometimes spend hours without mov-

"The Last Supper." Who is sitting next to Christ?

ing the paintbrush in his hand, thinking about his next brushstroke. *"Leonardo has chosen the moment at which Christ declares that there is a traitor in the company. We are shown the effect of a speech on twelve persons, on twelve different temperaments: a single ray and twelve reflections (Burckhardt). The subject has been well analyzed by Goethe. It is clear that in a drama of this class, a kind of 'seated' drama, of which the subject is interior disquiet, surprise, anguish, it suffices to show the persons at half length; busts, face, and hands suffice to manifest the moral emotion; the table with its damask cloth by almost completely concealing the lower limbs offered the ingenious artist a resource which he knew how to use. The difficulty under these conditions was to succeed in constituting a whole with these thirteen figures seated side by side; the greatest weakness of the old painters was composition; each table companion seemed isolated from his neighbor. With an instinct of genius Leonardo divided his actors into two groups, two on each side of Christ, and he linked these groups so as to imbue the general outline with a certain continuity, animated by a single movement. The whole is like the successive undulations of a vast wave of emotions. The fatal word uttered by Christ seated at the middle of the table produces tumult which symmetrically repels and agitates the two nearest groups and which lapses as it is communicated to the two groups farther removed."*

That simple? Surely not. In the opinion of many researchers, Da Vinci's works are precisely that: encrypted messages charged with symbols in which nothing has been placed at random and everything has a significant meaning. Just by looking at the time-worn painting we notice, for example, that the person sitting to the right of Jesus, allegedly the "official beloved disciple" John, actually seems to be a woman, given the soft features and daintiness. Could it be Mary Magdalene? We are speaking about the Last Supper, the moment when the Rabbi from Galilee says farewell to His disciples. Many people think that, if the prostitute according to the bible really carried the *Holy Blood,* i.e. Christ's bloodline, then in this scene Da Vinci aims to show her as the elusive Holy Grail, the companion of a condemned man who carries the seed of the holy lineage in her womb.

However, there is more to it. Some researchers believe they can see the representation of the Zodiac in this scene. Just like the signs of the Zodiac which are grouped in threes depending on the element with which they are associated—water, fire, earth, and air—the apostles are positioned as such with the radiating light in the middle, i.e. the Sun, in this case, Jesus. Therefore, we are dealing with a piece with not only an esoteric and "religious," but also astrological content, thus proving the depth of the Florentine artist's multidisciplinary knowledge.

We could discuss at length Dan Brown's analysis of this masterpiece in his book, in terms of the symbolism contained therein, with the "wife" sitting to the right of Jesus Christ, carrying His seed. However, we must press on...

Leonardo da Vinci died in the French town of Cloux on May 2, 1519, taking too many secrets with him to the grave; indeed, those same secrets that were partly hidden in some of his exceptional paintings.

Like many others, he was a searcher who achieved knowledge that was out of the reach of the rest of the people, whether because of its unknown or inconvenient nature we do not know. The fact is that he discovered a mystery that was being hunted in other parts of the world.

The Holy Kingdom—1498 AD

MOVING ALONG AT AN UNHURRIED GAIT, BISHOP ALONSO SLOWLY YET INEX-
ORABLY DRAGGED HIS FULL-LENGTH DRESS along in the muddy water that
ran down Calle Valparaíso. It was not his first time in this sacred city,
home to a mixture of bandits, highwaymen—who took refuge in the
nearby Sierra Morena Mountains, *Marranos*—Jewish converts who
refused to let their ancient traditions die and who hid from the fierce
gaze of the inquisitors, and the searchers—those who knew the history
of heresies that filled that small region of Western Andalusia.

That man of sober appearance, God's minister who had received the
support of the monarch to the extent of being invited to spend the rest
of his days in the King's comfortable and rather dissolute Court, rejected such lavish privileges and chose to "take shelter" in that God-forsak-
en city, a region on the border in which the best thing that could happen to one was to lose one's money, and even one's life. However, he
knew what he was doing, having spent years of research trying to discover the whereabouts of the most sacred objects ever guarded, treasures that would give their finder information about God and His sons.
After years of searching, with more failures than luck, he stumbled
upon the right track, in Jaén, the Holy Kingdom, and so the last leg of
the journey began...

Journey into the present

ONCE MORE WE JOURNEYED THROUGH THE HEART OF THE OLD CITY. The
cold weather grew more intense with an unpleasant, icy wind, as we had
experienced on so many other early mornings in the past.

It started to rain. At the end the alley was deserted. Only the flick-
ering of a flame that lit the bar entrance gave signs of life in these parts.
It was the right time to get one's thoughts in order and to share one's
knowledge.

The firewood crackled inside the old brass stove. The casks containing high-quality wine rested miraculously on four fragile-looking poles. The rainwater began to gush with more force down the cobbled street, as happened that same night centuries ago when a bishop seemed to want to flee his destiny.

"Alonso Suárez de la Fuente del Sauce, the unburied Bishop who became wealthy during a period of economic hardship for the episcopate, by commissioning works charged with symbolism and cryptograms that resulted in an unfinished enigma, thus earning the name 'the builder,' of an occultist tradition that yearned to achieve the great discovery." This is how chroniclers describe the life and

The Jews hid their legacy in this region.

miracles of the Bishop of Jaén at the start of the 15th century, the descendant of a family of initiates who, at least until 1893, searched for the Table of the Temple of Jerusalem, as well as various revealing documents, in the labyrinthine corridors underneath the checkered cathedral floor. And they might have stumbled across something very interesting indeed.

The Temple looters

"And Solomon sent to Hiram, saying, Thou knowest that David my father could not build a house unto the name of Jehovah his God, because of the wars which were about him on every side, until Jehovah put them under the soles of his feet. But now Jehovah my God has given me rest on every side: there is neither adversary nor evil event. And behold, I purpose to build a house unto the name of Jehovah my God, as Jehovah spoke to David my father saying, Thy son, whom I will set upon thy throne in thy stead, he shall build a house unto my name" (1, Kings 5:2-5).

There it is in the Bible. Circa 930 BC, wise and powerful King Solomon ordered a temple to be built to the glory of God's holy name. Given the humility and willingness of the son of David, Jehovah granted him infinite wealth and capacity to build always with justice and divine wisdom. Thus, the temple, God Almighty's house on earth, had to be a place where wealth and symbolism stood out above the rest. Indeed, inside there would be worship of the divinity, and in the majestic rooms three objects invested with the power of God would be kept: the mythical Ark of the Covenant to protect the Tables of the Covenant, the Menorah (seven-branched candelabrum) and the Table of the Showbread.

The centuries went by and Jerusalem, the "City of Peace"—that is how paradoxes go—was plundered on many occasions. However, it was not until the year 70 AD that the legions of powerful Rome, led by Emperor Titus, entered the old city and looted the Jewish temple, taking with them the material and spiritual riches zealously kept by the House of God. In *War of the Jews*, VI, XXXII by historian and chronicler Flavius Josephus: *"And now all the soldiers had such vast quantities of the spoils which they had gotten by plunder, that in Syria a pound weight of gold was sold for half its former value."* He continues, in chapter VII, XVIII, by saying: *"as the most happy men ever get by piece-meal were here one heaped on another, and those both admirable and costly in their nature; and all brought togeth-*

er on that day demonstrated the vastness of the dominions of the Romans...But for those that were taken in the temple of Jerusalem, they made the greatest figure of them all; that is, the golden table, of the weight of many talents; the candlestick also."

This same road was used for access by the Roman legions during the conquest of the holy city and the treasures therein...

These were disturbing times. The constant invasions from the northern European Barbarians affected the already weakened Roman Empire around 410 AD. The fierce warriors led by Alaric the Goth quenched their thirst for battle with the blood of the defeated. The triumphant armies entered Rome, proudly raising their banners and weapons as they marched passed the Arch of Titus. On this, centuries earlier, as if an ironic reference to the non-existence of eternal power, the best Roman stone masons had engraved the reliefs that extolled victory and the final siege of the Holy City, as well as the final location of the imaginary treasure in the nearby Temple of Jupiter Capitolinus and in the Palace of the Caesars. Once again this fell into strangers' hands, but its real value did not lie in the magnificence of the jewels or gold.

The true value of this treasure was to be found in the depths of the souls of a caste of initiates who, knowing its importance, protected it with their lives. In fact, the belief, that secret story that has always surrounded man, was that its holder would be able to achieve Absolute Knowledge.

On the trail of the Jewish gold

ALTHOUGH THIS IS A POINT ON WHICH HISTORIANS fail to agree, the clues seem to indicate that all of the sacred objects of Jehovah's Temple were added to the so-called "Ancient Treasure" of the Visigoths, who carried it in their arks when they settled in the south of France in the 6th century, specifically in the city of Carcassonne. This was in the Languedoc region where the nomadic Jewish clans settled and which was called the Principality of Septimania, where before their final expulsion they must have hidden information that could have destabilized the Church. We will come back to that later on.

If we pick up the story from where we left it, from the moment when the Visigoths, "weighed down" with the treasure, settled in the famous French town, the traces of this begin to fade. Muslim chronicler Aben Adhari stated in one his mythical manuscripts that these sacred objects were taken to Toledo, *"countless treasure and plunder which included mysterious magnetic charms, the preservation and safekeeping of which determined the fate of the Empire founded by Athaulf ... "*

Unbelievable. But since history is cyclical, at the start of the 8th century the devout followers of Mohammed decided to cross the Mediterranean Sea and begin their conquest of Spain, starting with Andalusia, the gateway and land of unlimited riches. Thus, Tarik and Muza, the leaders of a powerful and well-organized army of Saracens, took the capital of the Visigoth kingdom, and yet again, repeating the events of centuries earlier, siege became a synonym for sacking. They tried to take the treasure to the East, and it was precisely then, during the journey from Toledo to the port of Cadiz, that the valuable cargo vanished. This was the start of centuries of speculations, research, hidden plots.

Caste of initiates

APPARENTLY, IF WE GO BY THE INFORMATION PRESENTED and the documents consulted, the mysterious cargo was hidden in a faraway place between the center and the south of the Iberian Peninsula, or, who knows, perhaps in the palace of a Muslim sheikh. Nevertheless, some researchers are reluctant to accept an explanation that they consider to be rather weak.

One of the most enigmatic events to date is used to support this theory, an event intrinsically linked to the present story, as we will see further on.

Aware of the danger approaching an Empire that was beginning to teeter violently, the Visigoths chose to build a strong fortress in the ancient city of Rhedae, in the county of Razès, where they transferred all the items from the well-stocked arks. In other words, Solomon's legacy never moved off French soil.

Of course, with the passing of time there must have been some trace left in the area to confirm such a widely-discussed and controversial statement. This piece of evidence, craved by some and spurned by others, apparently arrived. During the second half of the last century, the small town of Rennes-le-Château was the setting of a complicated network of conspiracies, treason, secret societies, and a mystery so huge that it could have knocked away the iron pillars of the omnipotent Western society. We will come back to the liaisons and astonishing legacies of Bishop Alonso in due course. We will just add that at the end of the 19th century he came into contact with the members of a secret society in Jaén and attended an important meeting with the purpose of "comparing discoveries." More than one piece of evidence has been left behind... in full view of everyone.

Meanwhile, at two opposite ends of Europe, separated by distance and the definition of the message, two of the most important events of 20th century history were taking place. In the Portuguese town of Fátima la Virgen, three shepherd children witnessed an apparition of

In the distance the silhouette of Rennes-le-Château stands out, a place that we will visit in the next chapter. It is worth it...

the Virgin Mary, and in Tsarist Russia Communism took to the streets, leading to the hopeful inner revolution of millions of people from all around the globe.

The huge door of the Cathedral creaked as it slowly opened, revealing an inside bathed in shadows. We went in. The fine, refreshing rain became unpleasant. The checkered floor reflected the delicate rays of light that began to filter through the dome windows, where the two naves crossed each other. Dawn was breaking. We walked with unsure steps. There was nobody inside, and the *Capilla del Santo Rostro* chapel could be made out at the back. The railing, closed tightly, prevented further progress. *"It does not matter. There it is."* The large chest of drawers went unnoticed in the ostentatiously decorated room. However, on the left and hidden in the semidarkness, we could make out the silhouette of what turned out to be the final resting place of Alonso Suárez de la Fuente del Sauce, the bishop who continued the quest much later in the year 1500. A character veiled in mystery...

The testament of Alonso

ALONSO SUÁREZ DE LA FUENTE DEL SAUCE, Bishop of Mondoñedo, Lugo, and Jaén, inquisitor-general and president of the Royal Council of Castile appointed by Her Majesty Queen Isabella the Catholic. With such credentials, no words are necessary.

He was born in the mid-15th century in the small town of Fuente del Sauce, Avila, hence his surnames. Son of Pedro Sanz Suárez and Catalina Suárez, his youth was not full of prosperity or money to waste. His family came from a noble background, which, although long-established, had not thrived for generations. As we see in *Historia de la Diócesis de Jaén y sus Obispos*, as the decades passed by, *"he held his home town in such high regard that when he was appointed Bishop of Mondoñedo—on 20 March 1493—as the heraldic motif on his coat of arms he chose a fountain with a weeping willow in the middle, whose branches drooped nostalgically to the floor with an air of grief and sorrow."* That simple? The answer is no. We should interpret this statement as the rich text that some researchers claim it is: the fountain and the Tree of Science inside the hexagon, an unmistakable symbol of Solomon.

Amid the green hills of the real Galicia, brimming with esoteric traditions, the young bishop came into contact with the region's culture of occultism and became involved in the ins and outs of the life and miracles of an immediate predecessor of the diocese of Lugo, Bishop Rosendo. In the words of writer Juan García Atienza, around the 10th century he *"possessed the magical characteristics of the initiated builder,"* ommissioning mammoth projects during a time when the episcopate was suffering economic hardships. Due to his tireless building work, along with an unprecedented altruism, he became the subject of a mysterious legend that lasted right until the end of his lifetime. With the passing of the years, the similarities between the diocese of one and another were inexplicable. Alonso was assigned to Malaga in 1499, but did not take up his post. The seat in Jaén remained unoccupied and, inexplicably, in the year 1500 he arrived at his new location where he remained for the rest of his days. At that time, Jaén was a border city without an identity of its own, and unwittingly protected a miscellaneous and aggressive mass of Jews, Moors, and Christians who lived alongside criminals and highwaymen. Nobody wanted to go there, much less those whose social standing and indisputable relationship with the king's court allowed them to be assigned to a better location. Nonetheless, Alonso seemed to be pleased with the news. The work to be done in a city where there was blatant crime on every street corner

Alonso was buried like a heretic inside a large drawer, forgotten by the Church...

was an arduous task, almost as hard as reconstructing the cathedral which was in an appalling state since the building work started by Bishop Nicolás de Biedma two centuries earlier was suddenly brought to a halt. The "apocryphal chroniclers" maintain that Nicolás began the construction of an enormous "book of stone," which would reveal the mysteries of creation to those who managed to decode the encrypted message. For decades the dilapidated church was a pilgrimage site for thousands of persons who could read part of the symbols. Of course, if these secrets existed, they would be inconvenient for somebody. And that somebody was Luis de Osorio, a prelate who rode triumphantly with the Catholic Monarchs during the taking of Granada, who ordered the building to be demolished in the second half of the 14th century.

Don Alonso found the devastated cathedral in ruins, and knowing that there was a secret hidden behind those ancient walls, he resumed the construction work to build his final initiatory testament: the Gothic Cathedral of Jaén. Unfortunately, as had happened with other predecessors, the building was never finished. While this construction work was in progress, it appears that the bishop followed the principles of those on the quest, and allegedly they found part of Solomon's treasures. The bishop took to spending all of his time founding buildings, which led to the conclusion that he possessed unlimited riches and earned him the name "the builder." Palaces, temples, bridges, fortresses, nothing seemed too much for Alonso's spending spree. His only requirement—a mysterious one at that—was that his coat of arms be carved on the buildings, a somewhat strange coat of arms as we mentioned earlier.

However, there are few doubts that he knew inside out the legend that lurked around the old city, where there was an intrinsic link between the tradition of the Table in Jaén, strange documents, and the Gothic treasure. Centuries later, displaying a divine justice quite unlike human justice, time seemed to reward Alonso, admitting that he was partly right with the discovery of the magnificent treasure of

Torredonjimeno, a few kilometers from the capital of the Holy Kingdom.

He might have gained his knowledge of this tradition through the cabalist Jews from the town's old quarter, the Chapruts, the owners and lords of the *Raudal de la Magdalena*. Aware of the valuable legacy bequeathed to him, he thanked his benefactors by planting the clues to the Solomonic mystery into his buildings. In his most magnificent building, the Holy Cathedral Church, his symbolic message became a testament. The only part of this Gothic building that survives today is the wall at the front. According to the greatest expert on these secrets, writer Juan Eslava Galán, this is a code that uses symbols instead of let-

ters. Thirty-five meters long by around eight meters tall, it is littered with Solomon's knot, the Baphomet or Templar idol representing wisdom, and various signs or mysterious marks in the stone. Along with the cloister of Guierero, it reasserts the centuries-old secret.

The search for King Solomon's Table seems to have come to a halt at the end of the last century, coinciding with the possible visit of the parish priest of Rennes-le-Château.

Tombstone of Bishop Alonso, buried three-and-a-half centuries later.

Some people claim that he spent several nights at the El Gorrión bar in Jaén, just a few meters away from the cathedral. We will come back to him in a while.

In this story of conspiracies and secret societies, we cannot leave out the lodges formed by members of the clergy and local nobility. If we pick up the thread of the story, in the second half of the 19th century a group of influential people were brought together to carry out this mission. Their leader was Canon Muñoz Garnica, a mysterious and uncommunicative person who, like his predecessors, became so rich overnight that the money from his foundations "grew as if by magic." This is common to all those who set out on the quest for these relics, who enjoy unlimited wealth that comes from an unknown source. Is someone trying to buy their silence?

The intense activity, as well as the several journeys to Italy and France, did not go unnoticed by the people of the small provincial town, awakening curiosity and suspicion among the parishioners. But what was it all for? It is likely that the answer is to be found in the countless hours that Garnica spent in the labyrinthine corridors of the diocesan archive, amidst yellowing manuscripts and dusty books. In the 20th century, some people took the risk of continuing the thrilling adventure, perishing in the attempt. In July 1968, a prestigious researcher discovered the last link of an endless chain; this was a long list of names that included members of the clergy, bourgeoisie, and even royalty written on the rough, yellow surface of a hundred-year-old papyrus. At the top of the page the following was handwritten:

The moment when the "heretic bishop" was buried in the cathedral.

"Those who looked for the cave." Did this refer to the cave underneath the Holy Chapel? As to be expected, the names Alonso Suárez de la Fuente del Sauce and Muñoz Garnica also appeared on the list.

Intense days charged with emotions. In reality, each new site involved an adventure full of contrasting experiences and emotions, but this one had been different. For a couple of hours we experienced the same sensations that those nineteenth-century researchers must have

Perhaps it is a signature? Later we will see that indeed it is, of a mysterious priest called François Bérenger Saunière.

had, knowing that they were hot on the trail of absolute knowledge, of mythical, sacred objects, and indeed, they seemed to be so close...

The day dawned bright. The streets were a seething mass of people of all origins and sorts. Amid this sea of people, the Renaissance cathedral, with Alonso's Gothic wall the only vestige of his great creation, stood proud and appealing like a huge magnet attracting attention. Of course, we could not resist its pull, and once again we succumbed to its charms. As we went inside, there was a sensation of fervent devotion and faith. The bishop of the capital city, wielding his censer, was conducting a somewhat unusual ceremony: the Supreme Pontiff was granting forgiveness of sins through his head representative in Jaén. When the ceremony came to an end, we headed for the *Capilla del Santo Rostro* chapel. The chest of drawers was in the same place it had been for almost four centuries. "Ironic fate, cruel reality." It was a contradiction that the great patron, a generous person with his parishioners who did so much for the province, was buried inside a drawer without an apparent right to a just and decent eternal resting place. It is as though someone, knowing what Alonso knew, wanted it to be that way. The fact is

A temple so full of symbols has to have a black Madonna...

that it seemed to be more like a punishment. Even though we were imbued with the magical ambiance that filled the temple, it was not enough to prevent our curiosity from awakening. To the right, on one of the sides that the public did not notice, a lady of advanced years was praying passionately. *"Who was she worshipping so fervently?"* Quietly, trying not to be noticed, we approached. It was a small chapel, with an even smaller painting halfway up the wall, illuminated by a faded bulb at the end of its life. "Vera imago Salvatoris" we read at the bottom. The strange elderly lady, sensing the presence of two odd "foreigners," turned her head and whispered: *"This is a saint of many miracles. If you light a candle he will grant whatever you ask for; a few years will pass by, perhaps two or five, but in the end your wish will be fulfilled. The sacristan has told me things about this painting that will make your hair stand on end."* This categorical statement left us stunned. *"Which saint is it?"* we hastened to ask. *"The world's true savior."* Then, with that aura of mystery about her that we had detected minutes earlier and as though she had revealed the greatest secret ever, she left. In any case, the Latin inscription that shone with a special light at the bottom of the painting declared emphatically: "The true face of the Savior."

Another immense shiver ran down our spines. Going by the encoded message written on Solomon's Table, the situation grew even more tense, since this allegedly contained God's true name.

The tenacious researchers from Jaén, Emy Jiménez Hurtado and María José Martínez Carrasco, fellows in this quest, ask themselves: "Could it be that the enigma of Christ's face is in Jaén?" A recently conducted investigation seems to show that this is not so preposterous.

We are in Jaén, the capital of the Holy Kingdom and the Holy Face, the place of 'strange' coincidences and special treasure, where the beautiful cathedral houses a mysterious painting. This painting depicts a person with fine features, blue eyes and red hair, with a strange inscription: "VERA IMAGO SALVATORIS, ADREGEMABGARUM-MISSA,"—"this is the true face of the Savior, sent by Abgar."

But who was Abgar? He was King of Edessa and Christ's contemporary, with whom he stayed in contact during the Jewish Passover when Jesus was arrested and crucified. They never saw each other in person, but the letters they exchanged during those times are mentioned both in the apocryphal gospels and in the public section of the Vatican library.

The divine sense of these letters was probably modified during the Council of Nicea, where Christianity became institutionalized and many actions performed by the Rabbi of Galilee were established as miracles; therefore, today we do not have the actual text of this correspondence.

According to these gospels, Abgar was the first guardian of the Holy Shroud. When Jesus died, he asked for the shroud to be taken to him

The true face of a savior who may have been "related" to Mary Magdalene, the bearer of the Holy Grail.

since he knew about the miracles linked to it, and it appears that when he touched it he was cured of all of his ills. This made him convert to Christianity and he ordered a portrait of Christ to be painted.

Both this painting and the shroud were protected zealously throughout history until the Templars and their reappearance in France. The history of the Templar guardians is well known, and after years of having disappeared the Shroud showed up in Turin.

At Jaén Cathedral we found clues that convince us that there was a relationship between Jesus and Abgar. The cathedral displays a painting which clearly shows a man dressed as a King, a person of color—Abgar was known as 'the black man'—helping a women onto a throne. Might Abgar have known about Jesus' and Mary Magdalene's relationship, and after the death of Christ helped she of Bethany to leave Palestine carrying the *Holy Blood* in order to carry on the bloodline? Could this painting be full of symbolism?

Could the true face of the Savior be the red-haired 'idol' that the Templars worshipped and which led to one of the many charges brought against them to cause their dissolution? Could they have prayed to the real Christ? What link is there between this painting sent to Abgar and the Holy Face worshipped only meters away in the same cathedral?

To sum up, those people who appear to have found treasure with spiritual rather than economic value which made them obscenely wealthy, seem to possess knowledge about a treasure that inspired fear and complete rejection by the Church, who openly and viciously attacked those who began the quest. Nevertheless, undoubtedly the greatest of all these researchers who saw his objectives fulfilled one after another had already visited this region, perhaps hunting for further knowledge. His name was François Bérenger Saunière, prelate of the small town of Rennes-le-Château, a place that at the end of the 19th century witnessed an event that changed the course of that other story, a story that people like Dan Brown have used to uncover an unjustly hidden secret. Whether or not you believe the information put forward so far in this book, the fact is that these events happened...in spite of everything, and everyone...

ACT V

Sacred
Genealogies
in Rennes

> *"Louvre Museum, Paris. 10:46 P.M.*
> *Renowned curator Jacques Saunière staggered through the vaul-*
> *ted archway of the museum's Grand Gallery. He lunged for the*
> *nearest painting he could see, a Caravaggio. Grabbing the gilded*
> *frame, the seventy-six-year-old man heaved the masterpiece*
> *towards himself until it tore from the wall and Saunière collap-*
> *sed backward in a heap beneath the canvas."*
>
> DAN BROWN, *The Da Vinci Code*

THIS IS HOW "THE DA VINCI CODE" OPENS, with the terrible murder of the curator of the Louvre, Jacques Saunière. The paintings kept in this museum are closely tied in with the denouement of the controversial novel. However, to avoid spoiling it for those who have not read the book, we will say that from the very beginning the author refers to real events to portray characters and to give overall consistency. Indeed, Saunière existed, but he was not the curator of the Louvre. He was a priest who at the end of the 19th century found some mysterious manuscripts inside two Visigoth pillars underneath the main altar in his church, which was dedicated to Mary Magdalene, no less. The contents of these manuscripts may have been of great significance based on the events that subsequently unfolded. Saunière—the priest—also travelled to Paris and was in the Louvre with the curator, and even bought three facsimile copies of paintings...which might have contained an encoded message.

Moreover, just as our story features strange manuscripts that we will speak about later on, Brown tells us: *"According to lore, the brotherhood had created a map of stone—a clef de voûte... or keystone—an engraved tablet that revealed the final resting place of the brotherhood's greatest secret...information so powerful that its protection was the reason for the brotherhood's very existence (...) Each had told Silas the exact same thing—that the keystone was ingeniously hidden at a precise location inside one of Paris's ancient churches—the Eglise de Saint-Sulpice."* This is the same church where the prelate in our story studied in his youth and where he subsequently arrived with the mysterious manuscripts, coming into contact with the prior, Abbot Bieil, and his nephew, Emile Hoffet, a member of some of Paris' secret societies. We will make just one observation, which is that once these manuscripts had been "decoded," one of words that appeared most frequently was "Sion."

Strange sacred genealogies, attacks on the Church, works of art charged with symbols, tombs where the bodies of important figures lay, and a curious society called the Priory of Sion...these are all elements of a story that must sound familiar. However, in this case it is not the famous "Da Vinci Code", but stark reality, in which Abbot François Bérenger Saunière plays the leading role. The same reality that sometimes, increasingly, is stranger than fiction. This is how it all happened.

Father Bérenger, architect and protagonist of a story like no other.

A humble priest from the country

THE SCENE THAT UNFOLDS BEFORE THE EYES OF THE VISITOR who arrives in these parts is breathtaking. Standing up high, almost tearing the white veil of clouds, is Rennes-le-Château, placed at random and boldly overlooking the masses of rock that rise nearby. It is a village in the foothills of the Pyrenees, where the seasons are extreme and the turbulent history is marked by tears and blood.

A few kilometers away, next to that fortress that achieved great glories in the past, our protagonist was born, on April 11, 1852. The young Saunière, who came from Montazels, soon found out that the large expanse of land that culminated in the upper mountains had seen strong armies pass through, people who had come from afar and who planted treasures in the region, leaving in their wake fortresses in ruins, legends with elements of truth in them, countless superstitions, and part of a heretical history that refused to disappear. His vocation as a priest started as a child, he himself saying that he was born with inner God consciousness. This gave him a quick and well-aimed introduction to culture, to books that contained secrets of the hermetic tradition, and he did not take long to realize that he was destined to take up a clearly defined quest.

The eldest of seven brothers and sisters, he had to take care of the needs of a humble family who earned enough to eat, and little more. At the age of 20 he finally joined the seminary, fulfilling a dream that he had carried with him throughout his short existence: to embrace faith in Christ ...and in "his Church?" That was another kettle of fish.

In 1879 he was finally ordained in the church of Saint-Sulpice, Paris, where he struck up a strong friendship with Abbot Bieil, at that time one of his mentors who was aware of Saunière's aspirations. The priest soon saw that his pupil could go very far with his charisma and excessive curiosity, predicting that he would reach the upper echelons of the Church quickly. However, this rise to power was hampered by a strong and outspoken personality. He was vicar in Alet for a while, held the title of curate in the village of Clat, and spent three years in the seminary of Narbonne where he gave classes to future priests before finally being "exiled" to the village of Rennes. There is no other way of describing it, at least any other person would have taken it that way, but not Saunière, who at last saw his plans taking shape.

He arrived at a village whose only access was a winding path and where there were only one hundred inhabitants left. Of course, these people had no church in which to take refuge, not even from the rain, since the building dedicated to Mary Magdalene was falling to pieces. However, this did not prevent that "initiate" from arriving, carrying many hopes and no money whatsoever.

The historical site had succumbed to the passing of the centuries. That imposing city, which had ruled the Razès region in which more

Entrance to the mysterious village, a place that has become a temple for heterodox people. Indeed, there is no shortage of reasons for this ...

than thirty thousand people lived together in peace—at least when they were not fighting among themselves—had been reduced to nothing. Aereda, as the village was called, had seen its best days, especially after the House of Trastamara of Aragón decided to make a bloody visit to this region. During the second half of the 14th century the decline began. The village had been marked by Athaulf's armies, the strategies employed by Blanchefort's Knights, the dreams of the Cathars of Languedoc, the riches hoarded by misers, and the conspiracies plotted by the descendants of the Sicambrians. And altogether, the secrets of one and another.

But this was the least of it. A first glance at his new residence convinced him to rent a room from Alexandrine Marrot, a local. In Gérard de Sède's publication *L'Or de Rennes*, the author describes the curator's financial situation with a wealth of detail, stating that although at the end of the 19th century the state paid priests a monthly wage, Saunière's money was withdrawn after he was listed as a "reactionary activist" when he gave an unsuccessful pre-election speech. In the words of De Sède, Saunière, living in harsh poverty, wrote the following in an account book: "Money I owe to Alexandrine Marrot—Year 1890, July-August: food and bread, 25 francs. In total, over sixteen months, 90 francs expenditure and 2 francs income. Secret funds: 80.25 francs."

Secret funds? The mysteries are beginning to reveal themselves.

Being such an inquisitive person, bursting with life and thirsty for knowledge, that small world began to suffocate him. Although he satisfied his desires for knowledge by learning unlikely languages, the months went by and he began to feel the effects of the sentence imposed on him by the government, which in a way had affected his reputation with the politicians and his superiors at the Church. He did not have any means and he was struggling to make ends meet in a house in which more cracks appeared every day, teaching God's word in a church whose vault looked increasingly like the vault of heaven, and in which vermin and bugs roamed freely among the worm-eaten pews and the ruined sculptures.

He could not carry on like that, so he moved to an ancestral home made of stone, somewhat more solid than his last house, and began to devise a strategy that ended up turning him into one of the most "powerful" and influential men in Europe. All of this was thanks to an astonishing discovery.

Manuscripts underneath the altar

READY TO FACE UP TO THE CHANGES THAT WERE DRAWING NEAR, he decided to renovate his church. This could not continue in its sorry state of neglect, and although his relationship with the village council was not very friendly, the heads of Rennes were not completely averse to the priest's initiative, since in reality the only thing he was doing was watching over the people's spiritual heritage.

The flagstone underneath the altar was lifted carefully. Beneath there were engravings of knights on horseback, carrying a child and a scepter…

Since times were becoming somewhat turbulent, and in spite of not having sufficient income, he decided to employ a young servant girl who was not yet 20 years old. Her name was Marie Denarnaud, and over the years she became Saunière's loyal friend—in short, the "confessor's confidante," the only person who knew the prelate's last secret.

In 1891, with 600 francs borrowed from Father Pons, an old priest of Rennes, and 1,400 from the consistory, the abbot set about the task in hand. There was lots of work to do...and he was about to be overtaken by events.

Night had fallen and inside the church a faint light from an oil lamp illuminated those present. Saunière carefully studied the two workmen's every movement. Their job was indeed extremely important, since they were lifting up the flagstone that served as the main altar. The state of it did not allow for too many sudden movements.

In the picture, the "Knight's Flagstone" from the Merovingian period and of great importance in this story, as remains to be seen...

Once they had carefully laid the slab on the cold floor, a look of surprise came over the faces of the two workers. *"Silence. No one must find out,"* declared the priest, unable to bring his nerves under control. Underneath the heavy stone platform several leaves of fern fell to the floor. The two pillars that were holding it up were hollow! And not only that, but inside one of them they could make out something that resembled some tubes covered with worn and strong-smelling leather.

The wind beat against the church windows, and the cold, sinister night did not invite a walk around the surrounding area, even less so around the graveyard. During those early hours, something important was happening inside the church of Rennes, and Saunière was fully aware of it. Removing the dirt with some force, they managed to extract the two tubes. Inside, oblivious to the passing of time, there were several yellow parchments, covered with mildew and containing text that, at a glance, did not seem to make much sense.

According to Michael Baigent, Richard Leigh, and Henry Lincoln in their book *Holy Blood, Holy Grail*: "*it is said that two of the parchments were genealogies, one dating from 1244 and the other from 1644. Apparently, the other two documents had been written in the 1780s by one of Saunière's predecessors, Abbot Antoine Bigou, and they seemed to be written excerpts from the New Testament in Latin.*"

Parchments were discovered inside the pillars.

Whatever the case, seeing the stir that this caused in the village, and in an obvious ploy to mislead people, Saunière chose to play down the importance of the parchments, hinting that they were of little or no value. In any case, it was possible that an antique dealer might have wanted the rare documents, so he proposed to go to Paris. And so, carrying the parchments on his back he went to Carcassonne to notify Bishop Billard. The prelate's powers of persuasion were so strong that, after a few hours of explaining the situation, he convinced his superior. And not only that, but he had to seek the advice of a wise man of the capital, Father Bieil, Abbot of the church of Saint-Sulpice.

At daybreak, Saunière set off for the City of Light carrying a strangely protected bundle on his back, which contained the four parchments.

There he was given a euphoric welcome by Bieil, who without further ado immediately asked to see the mysterious manuscripts. At that moment the elderly man turned paler, if such a thing was possible. He saw something that made him lose his composure for a few seconds, giving way to a more than suspicious emotion.

The priest wrote down his discoveries on loose sheets of paper.

For a week, or perhaps longer, the documents remained in the priest's possession, while his nephew, Emile Hoffet, showed the abbot of Rennes Paris' different side. Hoffet, educated in Lorraine at the Sion Seminary School, *La colline inspirée*, had close contact with the generation of artists of the time. Painters, opera singers, writers, and esotericists made up his circle of friends; people of the arts from all kinds of social backgrounds, who without hesitating welcomed with open arms a humble priest from the country, the head of a village so small that few knew of its existence.

What did these inaccessible groups, mainly members of secret societies, see in Saunière for them to accept him as one of them? Did they perhaps know the content of the mysterious manuscripts? Little is known about this episode of the prelate's life, except that it was not the last time that he was seen with these and other persons of higher social standing...

Accompanied by Hoffet, Saunière was in his element during his stay in Paris. The city was an ever-flowing fountain of knowledge, especially for those who were thirsty. For that reason, or maybe another unknown purpose, he visited Europe's temple of art, in those times the best art gallery in the world: the Louvre museum. In this world-famous building, as well as speaking with the curator on several occasions, he bought copies of paintings that did not seem to be linked to each other in any way. These paintings were a portrait of Pope St. Celestine V; Tenier's "Saint Anthony"; and finally Poussin's "The Shepherds of Arcadia." The last turned out to be highly significant, since it represents three shepherds looking at a large tomb on which there is an inscription that reads *Et in Arcadia ego*—"I am also in Arcadia"—set in a scene familiar to the priest of Rennes.

But why did he buy those reproductions? What secret did they hide? Have patience, for we are getting there.

What is evident is that Saunière's first experience of Paris was positive in every way. There are many claims that during those times he met the opera singer Emma Calvé, a fully-fledged member of the "Groupe Indépendant d'Etudes Esotériques" founded by the occultist Papus, with whom he may have engaged in amorous pursuits. It is more than likely that the opera diva visited him in his house in Rennes-le-Château. Years earlier, his fellow countrymen put up a sign near the spot where they usually arranged to meet, indicating the direction to "Lovers' Fountain."

It was time to leave Paris and go home. His manuscripts stayed there, since there is no evidence that they were returned to him, at least not all of them. In fact, some time later, Monsignor Billard went to Bieil's home to reproach him for their content, but he paid no heed.

Before reaching Rennes, he stopped off again at Carcassonne, where the aforementioned Bishop was quite prepared to give 2,000 francs to settle the disobedient priest's debt with the council, and just like that, Saunière set off for his "headquarters."

Emma Calvé was quite a celebrity in those times, closely linked to secret cults, who fell inexplicably in love with Saunière.

Back in the village, he continued with the church's renovation, but not before paying back the money owed which, if the reader remembers, amounted to 1,200 francs. When asked by the mayor about the parchments, Saunière replied: *"We have received a good price for them..."* A mere bagatelle.

This time he did have money to spend, and the surprises did not take long to emerge. When the huge flagstone that covered the surface underneath the two pillars was moved, it was discovered that the underside bore a depiction of two knights. At a glance, the "Knight's Flagstone," as it was quickly named, dated from the Templar period. Indeed, the engraving was very similar to the Order's famous seal, a clear reference to the vow of poverty taken by the warrior monks. This was not surprising, seeing that this same region belonged to the sixth Grand Master of the Order of the Poor Knights of Christ and the Temple of Solomon, Bertrand de Blanchefort, whose castle stood in the distance. Later datings produced more convincing results, placing it several centuries earlier at the beginning of the Carolingian dynasty, and even in the 6th century AD during the Merovingian hegemony. The latter are intrinsically linked to this story, as we have seen and as we will confirm later on. One of the knights was carrying the delicate figure of a child in one hand and a scepter in the other. Who was that child? Also, a few meters below there was a pot containing various riches—gold coins and jewels which probably belonged to a burial of *misers*, a Turkish people who entered Europe in the mid-6th century—and the bones of at least two corpses.

"L'Or de Rennes"

IT WAS NOT LONG BEFORE SAUNIÈRE'S SUPERIORS, especially Bishop Felix-Arsene Billard, caught on to the strange behavior and wild life that their pupil had begun to lead. Seized by an uncontrollable desire to build no matter what, soon he set about repairing the pitiful road, which was really more of a mountain path, that led to the village. Was he expecting someone important? This is more than likely... however, things did not stop there. At a time when the Church was overwhelmed with debts and was dependent on donations from the faithful to keep up its good name, Bérenger began to spend ludicrous amounts of money, quite unusual for a humble priest like him, from a village in the highlands. Indeed, his income, which seemed to grow "as if by magic," came from other sources.

It was these newfound riches that he used to finish the Church of Mary Magdalene, which at the end of the 19th century far surpassed the previous temple. Constantly under Saunière's watchful gaze, the workmen spent months stuck inside those historic walls, mounting and dismantling at their master's orders, positioning windows, etc., but not once did they complain. Overcome by an irrational distrust, next to the vestry he ordered a room to be built accessed by a secret door hidden behind a closet. From what was he hiding?

Saunière had a reputation for paying well and looking after his workers as few others would. Indeed, after positioning the Stations of the Cross, completing the pulpit, or positioning the statues, Saunière did not miss the chance to actively participate in the alterations, painting the statue of the Magdalen at the front of the main altar. We will speak at great length about the strange symbols that the priest left in his church by way of an initiatory testament, since this is the key to understanding the knowledge that Saunière manipulated, and the message that he tried to transmit to those who knew how to read.

Night falls on the church in Rennes. Saunière waited until this time to start searching.

At the end of the year 1897, after considerable hardship, the church was renovated and it was time to open it with full honors. The Bishop of Carcassonne visited Rennes-le-Château for the event, and cannot have taken Saunière's strange imaginative blend of garish and ugly styles very well, since following his visit he removed the village from his list of pastoral visits. Indeed, Monsignor Billard, who knew Catholic theology through and through, could not help wincing when

The fierce-looking Asmodeus guards the church entrance. He protects the treasure kept inside.

he read the inscription at the church entrance, on the tympanum. These are the words of Jacob, Christ's ancestor, in Bethel: *Terribilis est locus iste*—"Terrible is this place"—a highly significant statement, as will be seen. Moreover, underneath this another inscription could be made out: *Mea domus orationis vocabitur*—"My house shall be called the House of Prayer." This was the final blow, since the Bishop, who we have said knew the Holy Scriptures inside out, was unable to understand the reason for that quotation, knowing that it went on to say "but ye have made it a den of thieves." Clearly, there was reason to feel a little upset.

Saunière did not seem to care much about his superiors' authority since, continuing with his frenzied building activity, he ordered a Renaissance-style country house to be built, which he called "Villa Béthanie" after the same region where Lazarus and possibly Mary

"Terrible is this place," where a priest attempted to leave
a secret related to Jesus Christ and His wife...

Magdalene lived. Recent archaeological studies have also revealed that Christ may have been baptized there, next to the church. As if this were not enough, Saunière bought several plots of land in the vicinity of what was shaping up to be an estate full of symbols, and in the year 1900 he began building what would be his last residence, the Tour Magdala, a two-story building perched above the ravine that runs through the Aude Valley. There he set up his room, featuring large windows and walls covered with a wonderful collection of books. Finally, not satisfied with all of these projects, he built a huge wall surrounding the graveyard, the church, "Villa Béthanie," and the Tower of Magdala.

At this point we should point out that the priest was spending money lavishly, and that money must have come from somewhere. The aforementioned author, De Sède, in his publication *L'Or de Rennes* says: "*as if he had inexhaustible resources, he gave free rein to all of the whims of his extravagant imagination. Not satisfied with having achieved the library he had been dreaming of for so long, he sent for a bookbinder from Toulouse who he*

"Villa Béthanie" was one of the most lavish projects undertaken by a priest who did not exactly bring in much income.

installed in his house, paying for all of his expenses during many months. He hired, also on a permanent basis, a photographer to take pictures of the most outstanding places in the region. He built up a collection of ten thousand post-cards and another hundred thousand stamps. He collected furniture, canvases, china. His two dogs were not enough for him, so he set up a zoo including fish, peacocks, monkey, and parrots. He fed his farmyard ducks sponge cake. Living in the country of cassoulet, he ordered his beans from Lille. These fantasies, as childish as they were expensive, still continue to amaze those who knew him in those auspicious times."

But there was more. On more than one occasion "Villa Béthanie" was bursting with people from far-off places, noblemen and politicians, painters and writers, and a mysterious character that his neighbors called "the stranger," none other than Archduke Johann of Hapsburg, cousin of the all-powerful Emperor of Austria-Hungary. What were these important figures doing at Saunière's house? Why did they go to Rennes, the small village that no one knew existed before these events?

In light of this information, we have no option but to think that the priest was in the possession of something, information maybe, that

In the garden he built this Way of the Cross, with the inscription "AOMPS" on the sides. What does this mean?

made him attractive to these elite figures, who did not hesitate to travel to the small village to share time with him, and who knows, some secrets.

It is obvious that Saunière's behavior, as strange as it was, left a lot to be desired. For instance, on several occasions and always accompanied by his beloved Marie, at night, when they could escape prying eyes and using only the faint light from candles, they would go to the graveyard and spend hours removing a few tombs. These acts were complete desecration, carried out by a member of the Church. Was that not the worst sin of all? What exactly did the graves in Rennes contain to make the priest decide to open them and look inside? It is difficult to know the answer, but what is certain is that he concentrated on one of them in particular, belonging to the noblewoman *"Marie de Negre D'Arles, Dame d'Haupoul de Blanchefort aged sixty seven years, died the 17th of January, 1781. May she rest in peace."* This lady was a descendant of the Blanchefort family, whose castle rose in the distance, at one time home to the Knights Templar of her ancestor, the sixth Grand Master of the Order. On the gravestone, next to a strange grammatical construction that seemed to make no sense—we will come back to this later—appeared the words *Reddis Regis Cellis Arcis*, which translate literally as "You are restored in the caves, you govern by the arks." What did that mean? Maybe a cave in which there was money or spiritual treasure? The person responsible for the carvings, Abbot Antoine Bigou, Saunière's predecessor and at the time confessor to the aforementioned marquess, left a kind of writing on the gravestone that could not be understood by just looking at it. Were they so interested in some buried bones? No. The truth was still far from being revealed.

Finally, the priest not only moved the gravestone while arguing that the graveyard was overcrowded, but in an attempt to remove all traces, he also destroyed the contents of both. However, this was in vain, since copies had been made of them years earlier by local archaeologists and published in the "Buletin de la Société des études scientifiques de l'Aude." So much effort for nothing.

What was written on the manuscripts?

DECADES PASSED BEFORE THE Rennes-le-Château mystery became world-famous through the BBC series entitled *The Lost Treasure of Jerusalem*, screened in 1972. The person in charge of the monumental project was producer Henry Lincoln, who was later joined by writer Richard Leigh and psychologist Michael Baigent. This first project was followed by the film *The Priest, the Painter and the Devil*, and a third television special called *The Shadow of The Templars*. To say that these were a resounding success is an understatement. The events that they recounted and their plot that centered around the small village in the south of France captivated all kinds of viewers.

Years of arduous and fascinating research finally bore fruit in the ultimate book for lovers of this subject, including Dan Brown, *Holy Blood, Holy Grail*. This was a revealing publication that for the first time presented arguments relating to Christ's life, Rennes-le-Château, Mary Magdalene, the *Sang Real*, the Knights Templar, the Cathars, the Priory of Sion... and those who protected their secret for millennia, with good reasons to take them into consideration.

Moreover, in this book the authors expound the results of research carried out on the controversial manuscripts that were discovered inside the Visigoth pillars. When these parchments were subjected to a decoding process, coherent messages finally began to appear. The authors state the following:

> "In one of the parchments, the words are arranged in an incoherent manner with no spaces between them, and some completely redundant letters have been added. In the second parchment, the lines seem to be cut short at random—unevenly, sometimes in the middle of a word—while some letters are placed conspicuously higher than the rest. In actual fact, these parchments are a sequence of ingenious codes. Some of them are amazingly complex and unpredictable, even undecipherable by computer if the necessary code is not applied. The deciphered message below appears in several French publications dedicated to Rennes-le-Château and in two films on this subject that we produced for the BBC:
>
> 'Bergere pas de tentation que Poussin Teniers gardent la clef pax DCLXXXI par la croix et ce cheval de Dieu j'acheve ce daemon de gardien a midi pommes blues (Shepherdess, no temptation, that Poussin, Teniers, hold the key; Peace 681, by the cross and this

horse of God, I complete - or destroy - this daemon of the guardian
at noon. Blue apples.)'

However, although some of the codes are discouraging due to
their complexity, others are blatantly obvious. For instance, in the
second parchment the raised letters, when read continuously, con-
vey a coherent message:

'A Dagobert II roi et a Sion est ce tresor et il est la mort. (To
Dagobert II King, and to Sion belongs this treasure and he is there
dead).'"

Incredible... yet true. This story is at last beginning to make sense.
Dagobert II, the last of the Merovingian Kings and the one who according to the apocryphal chroniclers descended from the holy bloodline of
Mary Magdalene, rose from the ashes in the form of a coded message,
in some ancient parchments found inside the church at Rennes. What
was he trying to say? That the monarch was buried there? That the
dynasty had lived on in this region? That his secret was hidden beneath
those creaking walls? That there was treasure buried underneath the
floor which was owned by Sion, the order founded in 1099 by Godfrey
of Bouillon in Jerusalem, the latter being heir to a line of Merovingians
who survived the disaster? That this treasure was spiritual, possibly
represented in some parchments that contained a series of sacred
genealogies, those documents that another order, the Priory, possessed
and of which they had become guardians? There are so many questions,
and so many possible answers. The fact remains that the manuscript
made a categorical revelation, and made a clear reference to matters of
vital importance in our story.

Let us look at the first translated message: *"Shepherdess, no temptation,*
that Poussin, Teniers, hold the key; Peace 681, by the cross and this horse of God,
I complete - or destroy - this daemon of the guardian at noon. Blue apples." The
reader will remember that while in Paris, Saunière bought several paintings at the Louvre Museum, one of them by David Teniers—"Saint

Anthony the Hermit"—and another by Nicolas Poussin—"The Shepherds of Arcadia." *"That Poussin, Teniers, hold the key...daemon of the guardian ... Blue apples..."* Although it is hard to believe, there is a deep meaning behind all of this.

We will deal firstly with Poussin. This painter depicted a pastoral landscape with high mountains in the background, and in the foreground several persons looking at a large tombstone, on which are written the words *Et in Arcadia Ego.* The mystery began to take on absurd proportions when Gérard de Sède, encouraged by an anonymous tip, claimed that he had found the strange place in the painting and, what was even more unusual, the huge granite tombstone, just a few kilometers from Rennes!

What ancient secret was the work of art hiding? What had the painter intended to represent in this?

Lithograph of the famous painting by Nicolas Poussin, a work of art that, like those in Dan Brown's novel, contains many symbols.

Indeed, few doubts remain when we compare the painting to the real landscape. Firstly, the tomb, and in the distance Mount Cardou; a little farther back the castle of the Blanchefort family, and in the background the village of Rennes... Perhaps Poussin wanted to show that "someone very important" was buried in that enormous tomb? Mary Magdalene or Christ's body, taken there by the Knights Templar, possessors of the greatest secret ever, that secret that went against the dogma of the Resurrection with one stroke of the pen, and which spoke about descendants? Of course, this is pure conjecture, but it does have

What remains of the tomb that Nicolas Poussin painted in his "The Shepherds of Arcadia." Who was buried there?

some grounding. The granite tomb, built relatively recently, might have been an exact replica of what existed in the wooded spot a long time ago, and which inspired an all-too-knowing Poussin. However, to satisfy the reader's curiosity, we will say that this tomb was ruined by a heartless man eager to solve many mysteries as soon as possible, and that, apart from stuffy air, there was nothing else inside. Nonetheless, some answers were indeed found in the recreated countryside, which were hiding in the background.

In *Misterios para compartir* (2002), the following was made clear: *"there have been speculations that it is a riddle or an anagram. By playing around with the 'homophony'—words that have the same sound form but distinct meanings—all manner of conclusions are drawn:*

-Arcadia: Arca Dei or Ark of God—Ark of the Covenant of which there is no record since the 10th century AD.

Of course, maybe 'ark' should be interpreted as 'tomb,' which would give us the tomb of Christ (...) When the Knights Templar were arrested in 1314, many of their documents and secrets had been protected previously. One of those documents was put somewhere 'safe' by the Blanchefort family, and later by the Hautpou family. This was the document that the Priest of Rennes discovered. What did that document contain? In fact, this was the secret location of a tomb, which had been protected by the Knights Templar from Blanchefort and from the Castle in Arqués, which was also nearby.

MARIANO FERNÁNDEZ URRESTI AND LORENZO FERNÁNDEZ BUENO

ET IN ARCADIA EGO
This inscription would be an anagram:
THE TOMB OF CHRIST –THE BODY OF CHRIST– *LE CORP DE DIEU*
There was a tendency in the Languedoc region to delete articles and prepositions:
CORPS DIEU
But in Languedoc, the letter 'o' sounds like an 'a,' and the diphthong 'eu' an 'ou':
CARPS DOU – CARDOU

Mount Cardou—which was included in Poussin's painting next to Rennes and the castle of the Blanchefort family—was hiding a tomb, the tomb of God, protected by the Knights Templar and whose secret was written on the parchments, and of which certain movements were also linked to the Templars and the Priory of Sion, which they wanted to pass on by using symbolic geometry.

Bérenger had discovered the real tomb of Christ and that secret was priceless, for all the gold offered to him."

This is a possibility. But the meaning of *Et in Arcadia ego* was yet to be cracked. Arcadia was a region in Greece where, according to classi-

Self-portrait of Nicolas Poussin.

cal poetry, the inhabitants led a "carefree and dissolute" life. However, it was also one of the places where the tribe known as the Sicambrians originated, the original members of the Merovignian family.

But what led Poussin to place a group of Arcadian shepherds in the French countryside? It may be telling that the mysterious sentence appeared somewhere we have already mentioned: the tomb of Marie de Negre.

In *The Sacred Connection*, Henry Lincoln reveals the following: "*In accordance with studies conducted in London, the documents that our priest found contained texts written in code with a 'double' substitution and transposition cipher as if working on a chessboard, with extra complications in the form of intentional design errors in order to plant false trails. These conclusions were reached without having successfully deciphered the texts.*

Nonetheless, these studies returned again and again to one vital and resonant sentence: 'Poussin holds the key.' This was the only link between the artist and the fact that Saunière bought a copy of 'The Shepherds of Arcadia.' I had seen photographs of a tomb in a pastoral landscape. The setting, I was told, was a few kilometres from Rennes-le-Château, on the right-hand side of the road that connected the towns of Serres and Arqués. Both the tomb and the landscape seemed to be identical to those depicted in Poussin's painting.

While studying a point of inflection between Poussin and his painting I discovered another important link. It is well known that Saunière's parchments contain a hidden message. There is a possible hidden complex geometric pattern to the letters. There is also a simpler and more important message in the inscription

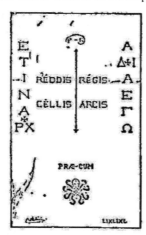

on the tombstone, which Saunière carefully tried to erase—without success, since it would seem that a copy of this tombstone had already been made. This was located in the graveyard in Rennes-le-Château and belonged to a great lady of the 18th century. She was Marie de Blanchefort, who died in 1781. The inscription on her gravestone was fully linked to the secret message in the parchments.

The two vertical lines that ran along the edges of the tombstone did not seem to difficult to read, yet they failed to convey satisfactory meaning. The text in the middle is Latin, as is the left column at first sight. The right column seems to be written in Greek: 'Et in pax' is what the former suggests. However, following Latin grammatical rules, 'pax' is peace in the nominative and is grammatically incorrect following the preposition 'in.' The right column does not seem to make much sense. Although all the text is in Latin, the vertical columns appear to have been written using the Greek alphabet. The key was very simple. All that was needed was to transcribe the letters E, T, Y, N in the Roman alphabet and the A stayed the same. Following this pattern, the P becomes an R and the X a K. The two columns read as follows: 'Et in Arcadia ego...,' i.e., the inscription on the tomb that the shepherds are looking at. All of the above suggests that there may be a key to the mystery in Poussin's

Characters engraved on the grave of Marie de Negre.

paintings." Remember that on the tomb the following sentence also appeared: *Reddis Regis Cellis Arcis*—"You are restored in the caves, you govern by the arks." Arks, caves, treasures...

Teniers also *"held the key."* He painted Saint Anthony the Hermit, a patron saint celebrated on January 17. This date is repeated throughout this story, starting with the death of Marie de Negre, and which is important as we will see. Saint Anthony was of Egyptian origin and was the founder of the Order of Anthonians. In the opinion of researchers such as Geoffrey Denizard, *"Before the Crusades, the Anthonians went to Egypt. They were searching for something: Saint Anthony's bones. It may have emerged through the hermits who returned to Europe via Italy that there were documents there that confirmed that the life of Christ was not only limited to the four Gospels. Bear in mind that in those times around forty Gospels or more were considered to exist. It is possible that all of these documents were in the possession of Saint Anthony the Hermit, given the power he had over the monks in the region.*

His disciples might have looked after these manuscripts, which were later passed down to the Knights Templar, who in turn went on to protect them. Thus, inter alia, *when the Crusade started against the warrior monks the latter were accused of spitting on the Cross. This may be true, since for them this symbol held no value whatsoever."*

It goes without saying that he is referring to the Gnostic Gospels discovered in 1945 in the Egyptian Desert in Nag Hammadi.

Evidently, all of Saunière's actions are laden with meaning or symbols.

Going off on a tangent, in spite of the proof, or rather, the documents, some

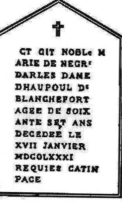

CT GIT NOBL⋅ M
ARIE DE NEGR⋅
DARLES DAME
DHAUPOUL D⋅
BLANCHEFORT
AGEE DE SOIX
ANTE SET ANS
DECEDEE LE
XVII JANVIER
MDCOLXXXI
REQUIES CATIN
PACE

Gravestone of Marie de Negre, with a legend engraved on it.

people intended to put an end to the Rennes myth, attempting to provide an explanation for each of the mysteries. A difficult, if not impossible, task. Among them was the chronicler René Descadeillas, who years earlier published the following report entitled "Notice sur Rennes-le-Château et l'abbé Saunière:"

"When on June 1, 1885, Priest Bérenger Saunière was posted to Rennes, there were around 300 parishioners in the village. At that time, aged 33 years, Saunière came from a small village in Pays de Sault in the Pyrenees, in Clat to be precise, near the Ariège region. He was born on April 11, 1852, in Montazels, a village near Couiza in the Aude Valley, 5 km from Rennes. A young country priest, he was tall and well-built, in short, a true peasant farmer. He was considered to be intelligent and modest. There had been nothing unusual about his behaviour until then.

"The only incident that might be called unusual was when he stepped up to the pulpit during the Spring 1885 elections and said: 'The elections of October 4th, have already shown splendid results: victory is not yet absolute...These are solemn times and we must employ all our strength against the opponents: we must vote and vote well. Women must enlighten the lesser-educated voters so that they appoint the defenders of religion. May the 18th of October become our day of delivery...' When the Bishop was questioned by the prefect as to the truthfulness of these unpleasant events, and having answered the relevant questions and refusing to remove the priest from his ministry, the civil governor decided on suspension without pay for the priest as from April 1th, 1886. Saunière, displaying excellent behaviour, had his wages restored after a few months.

"Bérenger Saunière succeeded Antoine Croc, 64 years old, and before him Eugène Mocquin, 45 years old, two run-of-the-mill priests. When Saunière took up his post, he found the church in a very sorry state. The interior was dilapidated with part of it in ruins, and the exterior in a state of deterioration. The bell tower was threatening to collapse, the vault was cracking and raindrops fell on the main altar.

"The refurbishments undertaken concerned, inter alia, the main altar. Indeed, the church in Rennes, a very old building if we are to believe a report written by Diocesan Architect M. Cals, de Carcassonne (Arch. Aude, série O-Rennes), con-

tained a primitive altar comprising a stone table with the front resting on two square pillars. One of these pillars featured archaic sculptures. It would seem— and several official pieces of evidence still exist—that when the priest worked the entablature loose, he discovered a cavity filled with dry fern. In the middle of this there were two or three rolls, which turned out to be parchments and which the priest took immediately. He said that he 'was going to read them and translate them if he could'. The mayor, knowing this, requested the translation from the priest, and a short while later the latter gave it to him in person. The translated text seemed to refer to the construction of the church and the altar. It is not known what became of the documents.

"The priest also removed the flagstones and excavated in the earth. There are

Comparison
of the
countryside
shown in
Poussin's
painting and
the land-
scape in the
background.

witnesses to this event, an elderly man who was a boy at the time and who followed the catechism.

"A foster sister of the priest's maid, who is still alive, does not conceal that while Saunière was refurbishing the church he found a jar filled with gold coins. This is highly likely in my opinion, since Saunière's unfortunate predecessor, Abbot Antoine Bigou, a 70-year-old man who was forced to cross the Spanish border in September 1792, buried his savings there, as well as the liturgical objects that he wanted to save from future inventories.

"On June 21, 1891, the first communion was celebrated with great solemnity. *The priest had a statue of the Virgin Mary erected and blessed on common land in front of the church entrance, which he called Notre-Dame de Lourdes and which stood on one of the two pillars that had previously supported the main altar.*

"*However, Saunière was not satisfied with acquiring the site that he dedicated to Our Lady and which was opposite a triangular plot where the churchgoers usually stopped when they left the church services. It was, if you like, the equivalent of a public square. He asked the council for permission to use the land, to close it at his own decision, to build religious monuments there... On February*

**Marie Denarnaud,
the priest's faithful
"companion."**

15, 1891, the council received the priest's request and, refusing to give up the land which was and would remain council property and forbidding the priest from building shelters there, declared:

1° That the square, although paid for by the priest, does not give (sic) him or his successors any right to build and remains council property; that anyone who wishes will have the right to enter the premises, either to visit the monuments inside or to enter the graveyard.

2° That all of the entrances to this square will be locked by key, one of which will be in the possession of the mayor or his representative.

3° That once closed this square will open on Sundays and public holidays, as well as on local, regional or national holidays, from sunrise to sunset (arch. Aude, serie O-Rennes).

"*The priest had ordered flowerbeds to be built, forming a small garden, and he had decorated them with limestone that he had found inside the caves near the village. However, overstepping the council's warning, he had a small building erected on a corner joining the graveyard, which was specifically prohibited. Since* the council did not protest, Saunière set up his library and study in the small house. The public convenience was higher than the garden level and, as was customary in this village with a water shortage, the earth had been dug underneath the building to form a large cavity, which served as a cistern.

"On July 14, 1895, a fire of unprecedented violence devastated two or three buildings near the church. These were used as granaries and were surrounded by barns filled with hay. It was feared that the fire would spread through the entire district. The firemen arrived to collect water from the priest's cistern but Saunière, who had the only key to the premises, denied them entry. They had to force their way into the small house. The next day, Saunière went to the police station in Couiza and reported forcible entry.

"This time he went too far. On July 20, the council made a new decision. They ordered the priest to give up the presbytery and to set up his study and library elsewhere. The premises would be closed with a latch only and would be used to store the flowerpots. As for the entrances to the public square, they would no longer be locked with a key, not even during the night.

"Saunière had to agree. Shortly before, several of his fellow-citizens had made complaints to the prefecture. The priest shut himself away in the graveyard and began strange 'disruptions.' The following is the text from the two complaints that have been preserved and which we reproduce faithfully:

12 March 1895.
"Prefect,
"We have the honour of informing you that at the agreement reached by the council of Rennes-le-Château, at the meeting held on Sunday, March 10, 1895 at one o'clock in the afternoon in the village hall, we, the voters, protest that the so-called work that the priest has been given the right to continue is of no use... We ask to be allowed to repair each of the graves of our relations who rest there and that the priest has no right to remove, move and change the crosses or wreaths after we have laid them or made improvements to them.
"Signed...

From here on, the traveller realizes that the place they are entering, if not terrible, is certainly mysterious.

"The following is written in a more colourful style:

14 March 1895.

"Prefect,

"We are not at all happy that work is carried out in the graveyard, especially in the conditions up until now. Crosses have been moved, gravestones also, and this so-called work does not consist of repairs of any kind.

"Signed... (Arch. Aude, serie O-Rennes).

"Saunière was therefore ordered to cease turning the graveyard upside down. But what was he actually doing there? Why was he disrupting the tombs?

"Even so, he did meet the costs of repairing the graveyard. He ordered a wall to be built surrounding the site, as well as the beginnings of an unfinished ossuary.

"Meanwhile, the large-scale church refurbishments were completed. The vault

arrived and between November 1, 1896 and late April 1897 it was built. Saunière paid for everything.

"During the year 1900, he bought several undeveloped sites located to the

One of the strange manuscripts. To try out its broad meaning, invert the four horizontal letters of the signature. This is just a sample.

south of the church and the presbytery, next to the plateau. He also bought some old barns partly in ruins, alongside the road and facing the presbytery courtyard on the east. However, it should be pointed out that Saunière did not purchase this land under his own name. He bought it under different names, notably that of his maid, Marie Denarnaud, who was from Couiza and twenty years his junior, the latter's parents, and several persons related to them both. In 1901, on the site of the barns, he undertook the construction of a 'villa' in dressed stone and of questionable taste which he called 'Villa Béthanie', displaying Renaissance style. He also had a garden designed on an area of wasteland on the other side *of the road.*

"He rebuilt the ancient village walls following the round shape of the plateau. This wall was extremely thick, hollow and full of large cisterns.

"At one end he built a modest tower that stood no higher than the wall, with battlements and a sentry box, and two sets of stairs. This was the so-called Tour Magdala. In this enclosed space he ordered yet more gardens to be designed.

"He set up his library and study in this two-story building, which dominated the entire region, and he soon became famous.

"He ordered four oak shelves costing 10,000 francs from a furniture dealer in Carcassonne, which were put up in 1908. Yet Saunière no longer lived in Villa Béthanie and continued to live in the presbytery which, by a deed executed on March 24, 1907, he had rented out to the village hall for 20 francs a year, for a period of five years. The rent, to be renewed tacitly, would be terminated by right in the event of the priest's death or transfer. In order words, the council's plan to eject him did not have the desired effect.

"Submitting to the pressure applied—especially by his Bishop—he resigned from his post in Rennes on February 1, 1908, not before building an altar in 'Villa Béthanie,' where he offered mass.

"Was there a storm brewing? Saunière was uncouth, uneducated—his dubious taste displayed in his buildings and refurbishments are clear evidence of that—but he was cunning and maintained a mysteriously positive attitude. He was well aware that his strange conduct aroused at least the curiosity of many of his colleagues and superiors. What was his financial position? Where did his money come from? He lived comfortably and his cupboards were always full. After the year 1900 not a week went by when he was not lavishly entertaining guests. Rumours circulated about his various relationships: with Emma Calvé, the opera singer from Aveyron, who came to visit him in Rennes; with local politicians, Dujandin-Beaumetz, born in 1852, and Councillor for Limoux, Deputy for Aude continuously until 1889, who must have been Minister of Fine Arts. Other lesser-known persons included local or regional leaders of the Radical-Socialist Party, highly influential figures in Aude. Dignitaries, businessmen, industrialists... Saunière held no social prejudices. He treated his workers equally as well. Indeed, *when they arrived in the morning and at midday, they ate heartily at the priest's home and they were happy working in Rennes. Saunière kept a diary of the work schedule, and some pages of his entries still survive. I have been able to consult them.*

"There was a wine cellar in his home, which was famous throughout the

Let us play some more. By joining the last letters of the last four lines of the manuscript we get... By examining this, we will find some other encrypted messages.

region. The walls were covered with racks. When in any region a vintage year was mentioned, the priest ordered a few bottles. Thus, some racks contained 5 or 6 litres with a hand-written label: 'Tokay, year X... Each bottle cost X... F'. Lots of rum was consumed in his house. The food was good and the drink better.

"At the end of 1899, Saunière had been proposed for judgement by the prefect regarding a personal matter. The proposition resulted in a compulsory administrative enquiry conducted by the sous-préfet of Limoux. On October 16, 1899, this official reported the following to the prefect: 'Abbot Saunière in the possession of an excessive fortune. He has no dependant relatives. His conduct is satisfactory. He professes anti-government opinions. Attitude: militant reactionary. Unfavourable recommendation (Arch. Aude).' From that moment onwards, they probably wanted him to leave Rennes.

"It was known that Saunière often went away, sometimes for days on end,

without authorisation. *He was far-sighted, and worked out who might write to him while he was away, preparing his replies in advance. He had responses ready for the Bishop, the Bishop's Chancellor, the Grand Vicar, his priest colleagues...*

Poussin's paintings in which the Arcadian landscape makes several appearances.

'Rennes-le-Château, on...

'Dear Sir,

'I have respectfully read the letter that you addressed to me, to which I turn my full attention. The interest of the matter to which you refer has not escaped my notice, but it deserves careful consideration. Moreover, due to some urgent business I must postpone my response a few days.

'Yours truly, etc...'

"*Invariably, when Saunière caught the train at the station in Couiza, he always went in the same direction: Perpignan. Several witnesses attest to this fact. The indications are that his interests lay in that city, which was near but outside the Diocese. It is a shame that the distance makes it impossible to know which bank was his point of contact.*

"Furthermore, there were certain periods when the priest of Rennes received large money orders every day—up to 100 or 150 francs a day—carrying small amounts that ranged from 5 to 40 francs. Some money orders were sent to his home in Rennes. Many others were sent to Couiza, where he went to exchange them for money. One of the employees who gave him the money is still alive today.

"These postal orders came from highly diverse sources. The majority came from France, but many also came from Rhénanie in Switzerland, and from Northern Italy. One record shows that some money orders came from religious communities, which represented religious petitions. Abbot Saunière dealt in masses.

"Until Monseñor Felix-Arsene, Bishop of Carcassonne, took up the head post of the Diocese, no one demanded explanations from Abbot Saunière. The priest's buildings and his luxurious lifestyle—well beyond his means—led to all sorts of comments among the clergy and the high authorities.

"Later, Beauséjour asked him to justify the origins of his money. Saunière gave vague and time-wasting answers, which lead us to conclude that he was not prepared to divulge any information. A discussion ensued during which the only voice to be heard was the Bishop's, since Saunière literally played deaf. Following this, the priest wrote this letter to his Bishop, in a surprisingly guilty tone:

Entrance to the graveyard in Rennes, a place swarming with secrets.

'Sir, I have respectfully read your letter and I understand the intentions of which you inform me. Yet although our religion commends us to consider our spiritual interests above all others, and these are surely there above, it does not order us to neglect our material interests, which are here below. And mine are in Rennes and not elsewhere. I must say to you, no, Sir, I will never go...'

"Saunière, therefore, refused to leave Rennes, on terms that seem surprising and that change our ideas about the ecclesiastical discipline. Whatever the case, he was guilty of rebelling against his Bishop. This was just too much. Beauséjour obviously could not allow his authority to be undermined. On May 27, 1910 he was summoned before the Officers of the Diocese for having continued, despite the Bishop's orders and his promises made to the latter, to deal in masses outside the Diocese. He was summoned to appear on July 16, but did not

At the village entrance a sign prohibits the digging of holes...

show up. Given a peremptory summons on July 23, again he failed to appear. On this date, tried in absentia, the Officers of the Diocese passed a ruling, find-

ing him guilty of simony, excessive and unjustified spending—in which money from unpaid mass services seemed to have been used—disobedience to his bishop, a 'suspens a divinis' for a period of one month and the restitution of unpaid fees. It is impossible to establish the overall amount of money.

"Saunière, having obtained from the Bishop 'restitutio causae in integrum,' was summoned again on August 23. He appointed Lawyer Mis, from the barristers practicing in Limoux, and then Canon Doctor Huguet, Priest of Epiens, of the diocese in Agen. On October 15, Saunière, who had failed to appear, was represented by the aforementioned Canon Doctor. On November 5, the ruling required the abbot to go into retreat for a period of 10 days, but he was exempt from spiritual exercises.

A religious newspaper published the warning that Saunière could no longer offer mass as from December 5, 1910. However, shortly after he was reinstated in an order that came from the highest authorities..."

The house of the Magdalene

A REBEL HE WAS, THERE IS NO DOUBT ABOUT IT, and he also imposed his point of view, even at the risk of clashing directly with his superiors. It may have been the feeling of being well protected in powerful circles that led him to adopt this attitude, at times arrogant in the extreme.

This same knowledge that he possessed and that procured him so many influential friends was, at least partly, displayed on the outside and inside of his church. This we will look at briefly.

As we entered the premises, the grove hung over the traveller as densely as the air that filled the village: this is not a normal place, oh no. On the right, a small cave welcomed us. It was man-made, for Saunière spent months searching the area for stones of all sizes to carry out his small project. Skipping over other details, such as the Stations of the Cross in the middle of the garden with several unidentified letters engraved on it—AOMPS, which according to some scholars is the acronym of *Antiques Ordo Misticusque Priorato Sionis*—or the Notre-Dame de Lourdes statue standing on one of the pillars in which the parchments were found, we stopped in front of the church's façade. One author once described it as gaudy, of such crass taste that a spectator not versed in its history might walk straight past it. Yet this is where the strange facts begin to come to the surface.

It is essential that we try to get inside the priest's head for a moment, in order to understand his world of symbols and secrets. He left all of his knowledge in the sculptures, on the walls...In other words, stone follows the old principle of Templar constructions and it talks. Let us listen to what secrets it is whispering...

Opposite us, at the top of the wooden door were the famous words *Terribilis est locus iste* —"Terrible is this place." Of course, the message transmitted is not exactly kind, but it must not be taken literally; it refers to Jacob's exclamation in Bethel. The aforementioned researcher, Denizard, says: *"Jacob received an important revelation in which he was told that on the land on which he was lying and where the stone he was using as a pillow was to be found, the seed of his lineage would germinate. It must not be forgotten that Jacob is one of the most distinguished descendants of the House of David. Furthermore, the rock that he used as a headrest was for years kept inside the Dome of the Rock in Jerusalem, which became the headquarters of the Knights Templar."* This biblical character was Jesus' ancestor and therefore a member of the bloodline of King David. What was Saunière's intention? Was he hinting that the secret of the holy bloodline was hidden there? Or that one of the members of this bloodline was buried somewhere in the region—for example in a cave such as the one he was building at the entrance to the premises—or even underneath the church?

Mary Magdalene is a prevalent feature of this inscription.

As soon as we entered the church, a rather unpleasant character welcomed us. This is the demon Asmodeus, the guardian of the church and protector of the treasure. According to tradition, magnanimous King Solomon banished him to the desert after, having forgotten his seal ring, the demon denied him entry to the waterhole where the royal shipwreck was kept. Was treasure kept here too? Also, like many other statues in the church, he is kneeling on the checkered floor, which reminds us of the rule that applies when entering a Masonic Lodge, or rather during the initiation rite.

Asmodeus' head is supporting the baptismal font. On both sides it is protected by two basilisks, which according to Greek mythology froze anyone who dared to look into their eyes. But this is not all. Both basilisks, which look more like salamanders, frame a red inset with the initials "BS," Bérenger's enigmatic signature and seal, which if the reader remembers are also engraved on the cathedral of Jaén, on the Gothic choir stall, to be precise. The strange image is crowned by four angels, each making the sign of the cross, and the inscription *Par ce signe tu le vaincras*—"By this sign you shall conquer him."

At the back, John is baptising Jesus and underneath are the letters Alpha and Omega, beginning and end. Indeed, Christ before a master was an apprentice, and also had to undergo an initiation process. What is especially striking is that the gaze of both figures, Christ and Asmodeus, is fixed on a particular spot on the floor, where there are 64

The entrance to the church is full of perfectly legible symbols.

squares of a chessboard. Scholar Geoffrey Denizard claims that *"this statue is not connected to the Church's secrets, nor to secret societies, or anything similar. It is simply part of the initiatory knowledge that was taught in these places. It is said that in Egyptian tradition the devil's mission is to cause disorder among human beings. It is the Lord of Chaos.*

"Most people are atheists for two reasons: injustice, considering that everything is unjust; and because everything is in chaos. The latter is precisely the devil's responsibility.

"If you look at a chess set, it starts off with a perfectly orderly structure. But towards what does it move? Disorder. Then there is a moment when this disorder is

Asmodeus welcomes visitors, with his gaze fixed on the checkered church floor that is found in all Masonic lodges...

MARIANO FERNÁNDEZ URRESTI AND LORENZO FERNÁNDEZ BUENO

complete. So what happens? The expert chess player finds implicit order, because they know how to move the pieces. In this chaos, death sets off another type of order. The king dies, the ultimate sacrifice, and new order begins. All of this is linked to more general concepts. Basically, a chess game, the pieces, the moves, the geometry, the concept of karma...action, and reaction, in other words, expresses the dynamics of the move, yin and yang. If the game starts and I move a white pawn then there is immediately a reaction. I move a knight...chaos is being generated. I move another piece...There is no justice or injustice, just mathematics. And above all, there are rules. The uninitiated do not see the rules, because all they see is disorder and chaos. On the other hand the initiate sees the rules, the divine mathematics, the order, the architecture of the universe, the geometry...The set square and the compass. And the devil keeps these secrets."

We continued moving forward. If the decoration on the outside of the church was outrageous then the inside got no better. However, we were not here to pass opinions on Saunière's taste, which was clearly not too developed, but to analyze, for instance, the relief scene of Mary Magdalene under the main altar. It did not seem to hide anything but...*"At the front of the altar, Mary Magdalene appears with a skull at her feet. I get the impression that women were allowed to participate in this kind of Freemasonry, something very unusual in those times. The skull, book, and cave all refer to the so-called 'Chamber of Reflection' of these rites, a recreated cave in which the Candidate sits and in which there is a skull and some paper ...on this he writes his 'philosophical testament.' As the name suggests, before the initiate is admitted he is sent to this 'cave' to think."*

"With this testament they want to show him that he is going to die...and leave the profane world, hence the skull image," in the words of my good friend and researcher Geoffrey Denizard. Underneath, the following letters appear, taken from the mysterious manuscripts and which are yet to be solved:

JÉSV. ĐEDĚLA. VVLNĔRVĐ ✚ SPĚS.VNA. PĞNITĔNTIVĐ.
PĔR.ĐAĞDALĔNÆ. LACHRYĐAS ✚ PĔCCATA. NĞSTRA. DÍLVÆS.
✤

Saunière painted this scene with his own hands, making it clear that Mary Magdalene was in an advanced state of pregnancy? By whom?

What was the purpose of this strange iconography?

It was difficult to avoid turning our gaze to the sculpture of Saint Anthony the Hermit—founded of the Anthonians—standing on our left. Incidentally, does the reader know when this festival is celebrated? On January 17. Rings a bell, right? For many esoterists 17 to 20 January are extremely important days for their beliefs and rites. Indeed, they end on Saint Sebastian, the "secret" patron saint of the Knights Templar on the day when the winter solstice comes to an end. Another odd fact is that on the 17th, aside from the deaths of important characters in this story—Saunière for example—an "astronomical" event takes place, which is worth taking into consideration. At midday solar time, the sun's rays stream in through one of the windows causing the *pommes*

bleues—blue apples—phenomenon, three pinpoints of light in a triangle that move until they reach the altar. This is all part of a ritual that is celebrated in "Blue" Freemasonry. Let us remind ourselves of the manuscripts: *"by the cross and this horse of God, I complete—or destroy—this daemon of the guardian at noon. Blue apples"*. Is Asmodeus guarding the place marked by the three rays of light and where, *voilá*, the main altar is, below which manuscripts, skeletons, coins, etc, were found...and where Mary Magdalene displays her "pregnant tummy?" Is that what he was trying to tell us?

**Mary Magdalene,
the church "owner" and
guardian of all its secrets.**

Or that the treasure is different... perhaps more human? Whatever the case, there are constant surprises in waiting in this church where the symbols reach inconceivable levels. Behind the altar there are two figures that represent the Virgin Mary and Saint Joseph, each holding two children in their arms, who are identical! Maybe Saunière was saying, just like other traditions, that Christ had a twin brother, who was the person who died on the Cross? Could the Knights Templar, among others, have been in on this "secret" and, knowing that the Spiritual Being had not died, shown this duality on their seals, displaying two men on the same horse? Was that the vow of poverty taken by those who manipulated Europe socially and economically as they pleased? As you can see, there are far too many questions and only one person who links

Behind the main altar, Saint Joseph and the Virgin Mary carry two identical children in their arms. Is this the *didymus*?

them together: a priest who, needless to say at this stage, possessed above-average knowledge.

We will not swamp the reader with more facts, but will just add that when visiting this unique place, be sure to follow the trail of the fourteen paintings that form the Way of the Cross. It is a genuine map that reveals many secrets and which might have been planted with the aim of taking he who knows how to interpret it to a place not far from Rennes.

Father Saunière became ill on January 17, and died on the 22nd day of the same month, in the year 1917. Days earlier, his faithful maid,

The blue apples, a strange and studied phenomenon.
The priest left no loose ends...

Marie Denarnaud, ordered his coffin, although there had been no omens of the death of the robust and serene priest. The locals say that the priest who went to perform the extreme unction on the dying Saunière refused to do so until two days after his death. No one knew what François Bérenger Saunière's last words were, but one prelate, trembling violently, left the room stating that he had heard "terrible things."

Priest Bérenger Saunière died in this bed, when no one—or almost no one—was expecting it...

...and this is where the mortal remains lie of a man who knew too much.

The Priory of Sion

> *"The society to which I belong is extremely ancient.*
> *I merely succeed others, a point in a sequence."*

PIERRE DE PLANTARD, GRAND MASTER OF THE PRIORY OF SION

BE THAT AS IT MAY, THE FACT REMAINS THAT THE WORD "SION" makes several appearances in the manuscripts discovered in Rennes-le-Château during Father Saunière's tenure.

Indeed, if we look at the several lines of research that come out of this story, there is a more sinister possible cause of the death of our protagonist than just an incidental illness. Indeed, it is highly surprising that a person in a perfect state of health physically and mentally died with no warning whatsoever, and even more surprising that his coffin had been ordered a week earlier, when no one expected Saunière's death.

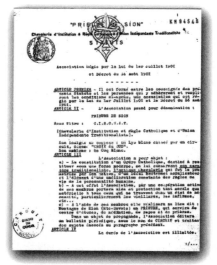

The statutes of the Order, the start of the investigations.

Enter Father Henri Boudet, a personal friend of Saunière's, in a way his mentor, and priest of the nearby village of Rennes-les-Bains. He subsidized Saunière's mammoth projects, including the church repairs, the Tower of Magdala, and "Villa Béthanie." In a space of less than two decades, this patron allegedly contributed the not inconsiderable sum of 15 million francs to Saunière's funds. Although he was strange in all respects, the son of a humble family but intelligent in the extreme, the two priests seemed to strike up a strong and long-lasting friendship. There are certain documents that state that even Marie Denarnaud acted as an "infiltrator" in Saunière's life, to the point that the huge sums of money always passed through her hands before reaching the priest. But in this story the mysterious Boudet employed another person. This was the

Bishop of Carcassonne, the same person who sent Saunière to France with the controversial manuscripts in his knapsack. If so, for whom did this man work? From where did these huge amounts of money come?

In 1956, a group of manuscripts began to circulate around certain social groups in France. These mentioned, *inter alia*, all of these possibilities, and they were signed by an order called the Priory of Sion.

The aforementioned year was in a way revealing for passionate detractors and defenders of this strange secret society. The first information came out in the form of official documents. However, in these documents there were references to the society's statutes and even mention of the names of some of the Grand Masters, who included figures as important as Victor Hugo, Isaac Newton, Claude Debussy, and even Leonardo da Vinci. Naturally, this news spread like wildfire, especially on account of the objectives of this mysterious group: to reclaim the French throne for Merovingian blood. Why all the interest? The answer is simple really. In the

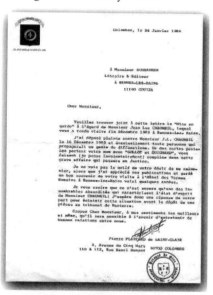

Letters signed by Plantard.

opinion of the members of this order, following the murder of Dagobert II and the entire royal family at the hand of the traitorous Pippin of Heristal—the founder of the Carolingian dynasty—one of the heirs miraculously survived and carried on the Merovingian dynasty. The importance of this person, who historians call Sigisbert

IV, stemmed from his blood, since he was none other than a descendant of the first Kings of Jerusalem. What does that mean? According to the Priory's secret manuscripts, following Jesus' death upon the Cross, His wife, Mary Magdalene, left Palestine pregnant and protected by Joseph of Arimathea. The Gnostic Gospels claim that she was "carrying" the Holy Grail, in this case represented by the *Sang Real* or Holy Blood of that group of political exiles. The members of the Grail Bloodline reached the French Coast a while after, where the descendants of the Jewish lineage merged with the heirs to the French throne. Thus, the Merovingian Dynasty was born, direct heirs—still according to this mysterious Order—to King David, and therefore Jesus Christ.

Priory internal journal.

An internal struggle ensued between the defenders of the faith, guided by Peter's dogmas, and the supporters of the bloodline, whose representative was Mary Magdalene, and resulted in the murder of Dagobert II and family. Nonetheless, as we have already mentioned, one of the sons survived and the bloodline was carried on until in 1099 one of the members, Godfrey of Bouillon, Duke of Lorraine, ascended the throne of Jerusalem which belonged legitimately to his lineage, even though he finally rejected it in favor of his brother who became King a year later. His descendants were "recorded" in some documents that were found centuries later in a Visigoth altar in the small village of Rennes-le-Château.

And so, Godfrey of Bouillon set up the Order of Sion high on a mountain, where the Abbey of Notre Dame du Mont de Sion was built. According to chronicles, this looked more like a fortress than a temple. And since there was a great secret to defend, years later—in 1118—the Templar Order was founded.

In order not to confuse the reader, we will state that this Priory of Sion appeared during the second half of the 20th century, and was said to have inherited the learning and knowledge of that older society, which became trapped in the end of a dark 11th century.

The origins

THERE IS NO DOUBT THAT ONE OF THE MAIN ELEMENTS of *The Da Vinci Code* is the existence of a secret society, which has been at the heart of continuous struggles, and which has been led by some of the greatest minds in history. Yes, this is a more than a juicy element to introduce into the tale. However, what truth is there in all of this?

Who were the founders of the "modern" Priory and what were their objectives?

As we have said, the "anonymous" members of this group were intent on reclaiming a throne, at first light fictitious, for the one who they considered to be the legitimate heir, and thus create and set in motion a kind of United States of Europe.

The names of the most distinguished members, their ideology, objectives, and "knowledge" were recorded

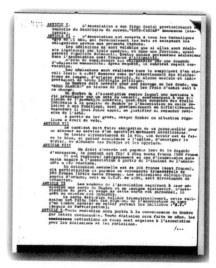

Laws… must be respected.

in a set of manuscripts called the *Dossiers Secrets*—"Secret Dossiers." These came out in public in snippets, providing information that implicitly showed that they had come from "privileged" circles, and which included cuttings of literary works, genealogies, historical records, and the names of the Grand Masters who over the centuries were at the head of the Priory of Sion.

According to these manuscripts, the leaders of this mysterious society—who consequently shared the secret that the group set out to protect, and fought tooth and nail to defend—had been:

Jean de Gisors, first Grand Master of the Order, 1188-1220.
Marie de Saint-Clair, 1220-1266.
Guillaume de Gisors, 1266-1307.
Edouard de Bar, 1307-1336.
Jeanne de Bar, 1336-1351.
Jean de Saint-Clair, 1351-1366.
Blanche d'Evreux, 1366-1398.
Nicolas Flamel, 1398-1418.
René de Anjou, 1418-1480.
Iolande de Bar, 1480-1483.
Sandro Filipepi, 1483-1510.
Leonardo da Vinci, 1510-1519.
Connétable de Borbón, 1519-1527.
Ferdinand de Gonzague, 1527-1575.
Louis de Nevers, 1575-1595.
Robert Fludd, 1595-1637.
Johann Valentin Andrea, 1637-1654.
Robert Boyle, 1654-1691.
Isaac Newton, 1691-1727.
Charles Radclyffe, 1727-1746.
Charles de Lorraine, 1746-1780.
Maximilien de Lorraine, 1780-1801.
Charles Nodier, 1801-1844.
Victor Hugo, 1844-1885.
Claude Debussy, 1885-1918.
Jean Cocteau, 1918- ?.

Some names in there sound familiar, don't they? Scholars soon shouted from the rooftops when they had read this list thoroughly. The fact is that there were three well-defined groups. Firstly, there were the most famous persons. It was unlikely that, after the extensive biographies that had been written on these persons, the fact that they were Grand Masters of an Order such as the one in question had gone unnoticed, in spite of the well-known esoteric concerns of some of them, such as Victor Hugo.

Secondly, there were the lesser-known persons, European noblemen, for whom it is almost impossible to find out details about their lives. And finally, there was the "scientific group". It was difficult to imagine Isaac Newton leading a "sect" of this nature.

Yet it is more than obvious that from 1956 onwards, and following the appearance of the Priory's statutes in the National Library in Paris and the *Dossiers Secrets*, the interest shown in the events, *inter alia*

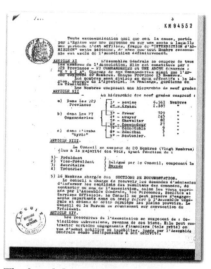

The breakdown of the secret society.

in Rennes-le-Château, gave an impulse to those who indiscriminately published everything that had happened in that small village set in the foothills of the Pyrenees. In fact, the events that took place there and Saunière's discovery, notably the strange manuscripts, unleashed a flood of information like no other to date. There was a tremendous eagerness to publish anything and everything linked to this story, not motivated by economic interests—at least that is what it seemed. Rather, there was a need to inform, to make people aware of another parallel story, of great significance if you like, the plot of which was said to come from confidential sources.

Indeed, in one of the *Dossiers* there was a reference to Bérenger Saunière as a "passive member" of the Priory. Moreover, their authors declared that before the priest of Rennes discovered the parchments inside the Visigoth pillars, two strangers representing the Priory of Sion arrived in the village to inform him of the place where these were hidden.

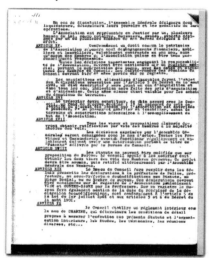

From then on, he served this society until 1916, when he quarrelled with them and inevitably left. Revenge was around the corner, which could explain why Saunière was in good health before his death and why his "faithful" servant Marie, who infiltrated the house under the orders of Father Boudet, ordered his coffin suspiciously in advance.

The documents were published in 1956.

Among the authors and researchers who got their hands on privileged information regarding this subject was Gérard de Sède, who, if the reader remembers, was the author of *L'Or de Rennes*. In this book he suggests that alongside Saunière there were people who manipulated truthful information, which was not accessible to just anyone. One of those persons was Pierre de Plantard, as remains to be seen.

The Protocols of the Learned Elders of Zion

At the end of the 19th century a document was published that categorically rejected anything remotely linked to Masonry or Judaism, arguing that the latter had set in motion an international conspiracy with the agenda of establishing a shadow government to control man's destiny. Had the Priory written this, or was it a direct attack on the society's possible objectives, staged by a more conservative group?

The aforementioned manuscript, entitled *The Protocols of the Learned Elders of Zion*, purported to show the foundations of a social and politi-

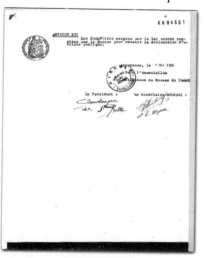

cal order led by a group of powerful sons of Israel. It fiercely condemned the plan that had been implemented in which the members of this group, the so-called "Learned Elders," established their government and leader.

Allegedly, this "announcement of intentions" in the form of yellowing script was drawn up at the World Jewish Congress held in Basel in 1897. It was next seen, bound and ready for presentation, in the hands of the Russian Tsars,

Plantard emerged as leader.

where it is a known fact that the Monarchs usually surrounded themselves with scholars well versed in the most diverse secret sciences, one of whom was Rasputin, possibly the most famous, but certainly not the only one. Also close by the Monarchs' side was a Frenchman called Monsieur Philippe, a celebrity in France's famous esoteric enclaves.

Other noblemen regarded his close relationship with the Tsar and the Tsarina with some suspicion, for they wanted to place their favorites in proximity to the imperial throne. This was the case of the Grand Duchess Elizabeth, who was intent on introducing an ungainly and taciturn man called Nilus into the highest influential circles. Trying to take a short cut on his climb to power, Nilus presented a highly controversial document to the Tsar that bore witness to a conspiracy, motivated by interests of power. The Tsar paid no heed to this document, not only ordering all copies of it to be destroyed, but banishing Nilus from the court.

The strange document seemed to fall into oblivion, until...

...it made such a forceful reappearance that hatred towards Jews grew voraciously. Even Hitler's minions—who firmly believed in it—used the document to hurl yet more abuse at this community. Of course, this manuscript displayed the intention to secure total world domination, infiltrate governments and secret societies to diminish their strength, and finally impose their despotic ideology. In Spain a few copies of this contemptible, libellous article survive. They are difficult to get hold of, having become almost antiques.

Grand Master of the Priory of Sion.

However, we have a copy, and we will at least share with you, by way of announcing its intentions, the prologue of the only Spanish version, dated 1936.

"As we present the famous PROTOCOLS to the public, it is worth inserting a literary work and a series of comments by way of guiding the reader through and illustrating each article.

180

"But given the special circumstances, for our beloved country is living the Spanish Civil War—and for the tragedy of this the Judeo-Masonic conspiracies are to blame—we would like the readers to make the necessary comments.

"And so the Protocols lie naked, unambiguously and without embellishments.

"We wish to circulate them since we believe it is of public necessity. For those unfamiliar with the Protocols, it is like opening a window and seeing an unexpected landscape with far-reaching and horrific views, never dreamed-of (...)

"What are, then, the origin and value of these protocols? Like the spark caused by chemical precipitates placed in a retort, the Protocols had the immense fortune to spark off anti-Semitic reactions, warning different communities of an imminent danger and publishing the plan conceived by Israel to secure its impressive destiny, the objective of its age-old ambitions: WORLD DOMINATION.

"In 1897, Zionist organisations held a Congress in Basel, at which the foundations of a program of conquest were laid, the extent of which was justified considering its success. This program did not only

In internal pamphlets, they claimed to be descendants of the first Order.

include the subsequent and ultimate aims to be fulfilled, but also announced the methods to be implemented and the strategic rules to be observed. At each Congress session, the 'Procès Verbal' or minutes was drawn up, called 'Protocols,' to keep alive the rules of these secret meetings (...)

"The conclusion to be drawn from the foregoing is that the 'Protocols' contain the essence of Hebrewism. Thus, even if they are an invention, it cannot be denied that their content is the faithful expression of Israel's will.

—Signed— A. M. D. G."

Aside from these pearls of wisdom, on the back page of this edition, before signing off the author suggested that the reader *"recommend this book to all of your friends and persons of goodwill who wish to sidestep the danger that, conducted by JUDAISM, the MASONS are propagating all around the world."* Quite unbelievable.

Who was behind the Protocols? It is unlikely that they were the result of the Congress held in Basel, since there are documents that claim that years earlier, in 1884 to be precise, other versions circulated around Europe and America. Apart from lengthy explanations of who were the possible authors, the texts seem to have been based on real information, which over time, or due to some unknown, sordid reason, was manipulated. In this regard, the authors of *Holy Blood, Holy Grail* conclude that: *"There was an original text on which the published version of the Protocols was based. This original text was not a forgery. On the contrary, it was authentic. But it had nothing whatever to do with Judaism or an 'international Jewish conspiracy.' It was issued rather from some Masonic organisation (...) which incorporated the word 'Sion'."* The famous Priory? Baigent, Lincoln, and Leigh go on to argue, quite rightly, that: *"The original text on which the published version of the Protocols was based need not have been provocative or inflammatory in its language. But it may well have included a program for gaining power, for infiltrating Masonry, for controlling social, political, and economic institutions."* The authors of this best-seller wind up by saying that: *"It is rather a radically altered text. But despite the alterations certain vestiges of the original version can be discerned (...) These vestiges—which referred to a king, a pope, an international church, and to Sion—(...) might have been extremely relevant to a secret society. As we learned subsequently, they were—and still are—of paramount importance to the Prieure de Sion."*

Remember that their agenda included restoring the throne to whom they considered the legitimate candidate. Who knew the plans of this society, who was intent on blowing them up at all costs? We cannot know for sure, but we can confirm that the founders of the present Priory of Sion—1956—even though at the climax of their existence they claimed the blood of the royal lineage of the House of David as their own, as "legitimate heirs" to the Grail Dynasty, had stood out years earlier for being fervent proponents of totalitarianism at its most nauseating.

The contradictions are glaring. Was the Priory an invention thought up by a group of madmen crazed by delusions of grandeur? Did they have any links with the ancient Order of Sion? Had it been founded to bind together conservative ideas that championed a return to tradition? Or, on the contrary, was it the answer to the growing interest that certain progressive movements in the Europe of that time were sowing among the people? All of these questions take us to one extraordinary character: Pierre de Plantard, a right-wing extremist and anti-Semite, who claimed his right to the throne of Jerusalem. Indeed, he was a descendant of the royal bloodline.

The hydra head

BORN IN 1920 INTO A NOBLE FAMILY who ran to seed, in 1937 Pierre de Plantard—the reader will remember that *plant ard* has already appeared in this book, nine hundred years earlier—was the leader of an organization known as "The French Union," which was divided into two wings: "For Unity," with a total of 10,414 members and "Youth of France," with around 1,600 members. In 1939, three summer camps were set up, at which extreme teachings were given; in other words, the young people were indoctrinated into holding anti-Semitic and anti-Masonic views. However, this organization was only a preliminary experiment for what was to ensue, and what was being hatched in the mind of this extremely frail-looking, imaginative man.

Pierre, clearly ultra-conservative in his outlook, soon founded the society *Alpha Galates*, an Order of Knighthood that reclaimed the esoteric and counter-revolutionary tradition of the *Grand Orient*, whose organ was a journal called *Vaincre*. He declared time and again that a

Judeo-Masonic plot was intent on gaining power. His obsession was such that he even sent a letter to Marshall Pétain, leader of the Nazi collaborationist government, to alert him to the matter. He deemed it necessary to "purify and renew France" in the struggle against this conspiracy.

His fascist tendencies stirred up the interest of secret societies, who discerned signs of danger in the passion that the youngster displayed each time he made a public appearance. Indeed, with these actions, he aimed to go even further, creating groups with similar ideologies to those which at that time were proclaimed in Hitler's Germany. In actual fact, this seemed to be more in line with the doctrine contained in the famous Protocols, than what in a few years time he ended up defending.

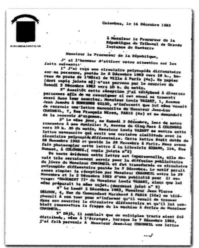

Pierre de Plantard resigned twice, and went back...

Nevertheless, Pierre de Plantard's ideological code changed over the years, although this may have been due to a perfectly-devised plan. The fact is that as a result of becoming intimate with the Plantard family doctor, Doctor Camille Savoire—founder of the Grand Priory of the Gauls and closely involved in the high circles of the secret societies of the time— our protagonist got caught up in an entirely different whirlpool.

In 1956 he founded a new society called "Priory of Sion." Yes, the same person who a while earlier had represented the views of the anti-Zionist movement, closely linked to the Third Reich, was now standing as legitimate heir to the throne of Jerusalem. In fact, in one of the aforementioned *Dossiers Secrets*, according to the genealogies contained inside, Plantard "emerged" as a direct descendent of Merovingian King Dagobert II. Amazing.

There was more to come. In 1981, Pierre de Plantard was elected Grand Master of the Priory in the town of Blois. This filled the "heir" with pride, and he symbolically prepared his "coronation" as head of the Priory in the same city where Nostradamus, in his famous Quatrains, predicted a Great Monarch. Symbols, symbols...and more symbols. Who was this man? Did he really belong to Christ's bloodline, or was he just a madman with delusions of grandeur?

In an interview granted to the authors of *Holy Blood, Holy Grail* conducted in March 1979, Plantard said off the cameras that: *"the Prieuré was in possession of the treasure of the Temple of Jerusalem, which some historians believe could be found somewhere between the Spanish towns of Toledo and Jaén, that is, the booty plundered by Titus' Roman legions in AD 70. The treasure, M. Plantard stated, would be returned to Israel 'when the time is right.' However, whatever the historical, archaeological or even political importance of this treasure, Plantard ruled it out stating that it was secondary. He insisted that the real treasure was 'spiritual.' He also implied that this 'spiritual treasure'*

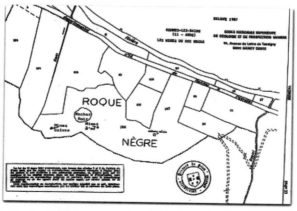

According to the Priory, near Rennes there are places that hide secrets...

consisted, at least partly, of a secret. In some unspecified way, this secret would bring about an important social change."

The lectures of the new "sapling" from then onwards became stirring historical and political speeches. On the one hand, he refused to reveal any information about an order that without intending to be secret, did want to pass through history discretely—at least recent history—and on the other, he fought tooth and nail to defend his rights as an heir, the last descendant of the Merovingian dynasty, and therefore carrier of the Jewish blood of the kings of Jerusalem. A delusion, anyway...

THE PRIORY ORGANIZATION

In accordance with the aforementioned statutes of the society, the eleventh to be precise, "The General Assembly comprises all of the members of the association (...) the members are divided into two groups: the Legion, charged with the apostolate, and the Phalange, guardian of the Tradition.

The members form a hierarchy of nine grades." These are shown in the twelfth statute: *"The hierarchy of nine grades consists of:*

> *1.- Novices: 6,561 members*
> *2.- Croices: 2,187 members*
> *3.- Preux: 729 members*
> *4.- Ecuyers: 243 members*
> *5.- Chevaliers: 81 members*
> *6.- Commadeurs: 27 members*
> *7.- Connetables: 9 members*
> *8.- Sénéchaux: 3 members*
> *9.- Nautonier: 1 member"*

It is clear that the organization of the Order was a combination of the severe Templar rules from the early 12th century and the fascist militia of Europe in the mid-20th century. However, it did not stop there. In the following statute, *"the council has twenty members, who act as:*

> *1.- President*
> *2.- Vice-president*
> *3.- Secretary*
> *4.- Treasurer*
> *5.- 16 members responsible*
> *for documentation"*

Broadly speaking, this was the makeup of the Priory of Sion. Too much bother just for a flimsy set-up? Who knows...the fact remains that Plantard knew too much, and that knowledge had to come out somehow.

In conclusion

AT THIS STAGE, FEW DOUBTS REMAIN AS TO WHETHER the Priory of Sion existed, whose members were descendents of the ancient Order founded in 1099 in Jerusalem with the objective of protecting a great secret: Jesus Christ's bloodline. This group might have been the guardian of valuable information, which not only referred to His fertility, represented in His child, but that there was a dynastic line that came from the Rabbi of Galilee. Now, there is a big difference between that and saying it is true, and going further, that Plantard and his followers were the "descendants" of those original Crusaders. It is more than likely that Pierre de Plantard took a story that began to look like a myth—such were the events in the small village of Rennes-le-Château—and used it to give free rein to his megalomaniacal personality.

Be that as it may, the subject continues to spark passions; the latest being those surrounding *The Da Vinci Code*. Whether this group existed or not, whether it was born out of a privileged imagination or the death throes of an ancient Order that manipulated vast knowledge for centuries, we will never know. Even if the Priory was a farce devised on the basis of anti-Semitic documents whose only aim was, in the pre-war era, to provoke bitter hatred towards the Jews, other secret and discrete societies are probably at present ensuring that the secret, the real one, continues to be protected.

God knows...or in this case, His children...